TUT·ANKH·AMEN

The Politics of Discovery

Front cover: Painted and gessoed wooden head of Tutankhamun rising from a lotus, in a metaphor of rebirth. [Griffith Institute, Oxford.]

TUT·ANKH·AMEN

The Politics of Discovery

by Howard Carter

Preface by the seventh Earl of Carnarvon
Introduction by Nicholas Reeves

LIBRI

Libri Publications Ltd,
Suite 281, 37 Store Street,
Bloomsbury,
London, WC1E 7BS.

Translations from the original French by Marius Nasta and Anna Lethbridge.

FRONTISPIECE: HOWARD CARTER, STANDING OUTSIDE HIS HOUSE AT ELWAT EL-DIBUN, CLOSE TO THE VALLEY OF THE KINGS, 1922-23. [GRIFFITH INSTITUTE, OXFORD]

ISBN 1 901965 00 7

Designed and typeset by Libri Publications Limited
Printed and bound in Great Britain by Biddles Limited
of Guildford

CONTENTS

PREFACE

by the seventh Earl of Carnarvon KCVO KBE

To discover a richly provisioned Egyptian royal burial is a privilege accorded few men—my grandfather and Howard Carter among them. Yet, on the 5th April 1922, only six months after Carter's workmen had unearthed the first step of the tomb of Tutankhamun, the fifth Earl was dead, unaware of the tomb's full magnificence.

Carter found himself heir not only to the awesome responsibility of safeguarding the tomb's fragile contents, but to a nasty political situation besides; while history has nothing but praise for his archaeological achievement, it has been less kind in its verdict on his handling of the petty jealousies pharaoh's riches had aroused.

With the publication of this extraordinary volume, Carter's own version of events during this troubled period, readers will be able to judge for themselves. It is not always possible to condone the man's method, but we can at least sympathise with his motivation: which was to discharge, to the best of his ability, the enormous task which had been entrusted to him.

Carnarvon

INTRODUCTION

by Nicholas Reeves

> 'No man is wise at all times—perhaps least of all the archaeologist who finds his efforts to carry out an all-absorbing task frustrated by a thousand pin-pricks and irritations without end. It is not for me to affix the blame for what occurred, nor yet to bear responsibility for a dispute in which at one moment the interests of archaeology in Egypt seemed menaced'.[1]
>
> *Howard Carter*

The discovery of the tomb of Tutankhamun[2] by the fifth Earl of Carnarvon and Howard Carter[3] stands as a landmark in the history of exploration in Egypt—for the burial's archaeological splendour, of course, but also because of the changes the find would carry in its wake. As a direct result of this discovery, and to a large extent Carter's handling of the politics surrounding it, the 'golden age' of excavating in Egypt would draw to a permanent close. *Tut·ankh·amen*, letter by letter, document by document, details how and why this came to pass.

*

Howard Carter's was an interesting career.[4] A man of relatively modest birth, he first visited Egypt in 1891 as a junior artist with the

[1] Howard Carter, *The Tomb of Tut.ankh.Amen*, II (London, 1927), p. xiii.
[2] This is the modern spelling of the name; Howard Carter's preferred spelling in the original version of this text, 'Tut.ankh.amen', though now somewhat dated, has been retained in the title and body of the present work.
[3] Carter (and A. C. Mace), *Tut.ankh.Amen*, I-III (London, 1923-33); more recently I. E. S. Edwards, *Tutankhamun: his Tomb and its Treasures* (New York, 1976); Nicholas Reeves, *The Complete Tutankhamun* (London, 1990).
[4] H. V. F. Winstone, *Howard Carter and the Discovery of the Tomb of Tutankhamun* (London, 1991); T. G. H. James, *Howard Carter. The Path to Tutankhamun* (London, 1992); Nicholas Reeves and John H. Taylor, *Howard Carter Before Tutankhamun* (London, 1992).

Egypt Exploration Fund which was then working at Beni Hasan and el-Bersha. The following year, after a spell with Flinders Petrie at el-Amarna, Carter went on to join Édouard Naville at the temple of Deir el-Bahri, and by the turn of the century, at the still tender age of twenty-five, he had been appointed Inspector-General of Antiquities for Upper Egypt with the Service des Antiquités. Although Carter's success in this post is now legendary, it all fell apart in 1905 with his unhappy transfer to Saqqara in the north. There was a fracas with a party of drunken French tourists who had been abusing his men, and Carter was ordered to apologise or resign. It says much about the man that he opted for the latter. For the next few years he would eke out a meagre and unsatisfactory living as a tourist guide, antiquities dealer and watercolourist, regarded by his colleagues as a failure and all but down-and-out.

Carter's break came in 1908 with an introduction—engineered by his old boss, Gaston Maspero, who still held him in high esteem—to the fifth Earl of Carnarvon[5]. Carnarvon had developed an interest in Egyptian archaeology as a way of passing the otherwise interminable months of winter exile he was forced to endure, on doctor's orders, following a serious motoring accident. Carnarvon and Carter, both loners, took to each other at once, and, with Carter to guide him, the fifth Earl's pastime developed rapidly into a passion and finally an obsession.

The pair concentrated much of their efforts on Thebes, excavating with good result in several areas of the private necropolis and

[5] Nicholas Reeves, *Ancient Egypt at Highclere Castle* (Highclere, 1989).

(OPPOSITE) THE FIFTH EARL OF CARNARVON, EVER ELEGANT, STANDS IN THE DOORWAY TO HOWARD CARTER'S HOUSE AT ELWAT EL-DIBUN CLUTCHING HIS CAMERA. CARNARVON HAD BEEN DRAWN TO EGYPT BY ITS MILD CLIMATE, FOLLOWING A NEAR-FATAL MOTORING ACCIDENT IN GERMANY IN 1901 WHICH LEFT HIM PHYSICALLY WEAKENED; PRONE TO CHILLS, HE WEARS BOTH A WAISTCOAT AND CARDIGAN BENEATH HIS HEAVY JACKET. [GRIFFITH INSTITUTE, OXFORD]

publishing with immense competence and style.[6] But their principal interest was royal tombs; and as soon as Theodore Davis—the wealthy American amateur who had been digging in the Valley of the Kings for more than a decade—gave up his concession, Carnarvon and Carter pounced.

From the very start, it seems, Carter had an inkling that there was something more to be found in the royal burial ground, and he set out systematically to find it. His first season of work, in an annexe of the Valley of the Kings known as the West Valley, was something of a diversion, prompted by Carter's purchase for Lord Carnarvon on the Luxor antiquities market of three carnelian bracelet plaques which seemed to have come from the tomb of Amenophis III. Here, in the spring of 1915, during a break from his war-work, Carter undertook to clear the sepulchre. The finds were interesting rather than spectacular; but Lord Carnarvon was sufficiently encouraged to invest in further digging from 1917 on, this time in the Valley of the Kings proper, which Carter determined to clear down to bedrock so that nothing would be missed.

Five years later, in 1922, Lord Carnarvon had little to show for his money. His enthusiasm had begun to flag—so much so that he threatened to withdraw his funding. Carter passionately argued for just one more season, at his own expense, and Carnarvon relented. Carter's instincts were good, and within days he struck gold.

The tomb first came to light in the central part of the main Valley on the morning of November 4th, 1922, when, so the story goes, Carter's water-boy, struggling to set up the communal *zeer* (water jar) for the workmen, noticed a straight edge cut into the rock. This, on further investigation, proved to be the top of a step—which was followed by a second, and then a third, until, by 4 o'clock the next afternoon, a tomb doorway had been uncovered,

[6] The Earl of Carnarvon and Howard Carter, *Five Years' Explorations at Thebes: a record of work done, 1907-1911* (Oxford, 1912).

plastered over its entire surface, stamped with large oval seals and displaying, in the top left-hand corner, evidence of two illicit entries and subsequent reclosures.

At the time of the discovery Lord Carnarvon was in England, and Carter, exerting every ounce of self-control, refilled the staircase and posted guards. He then dashed off his famous telegram to Highclere Castle—'At last have made wonderful discovery in the Valley. A magnificent tomb with seals intact. Congratulations'—and doubtless retired to the bar.

It was a further two and a half weeks before Carnarvon and his daughter, Lady Evelyn Herbert, stepped down from the train at Luxor station and investigation of the new find could recommence. As, rock by rock, the rubble fill was cleared from the entrance, the excavators' pulses began to race. It clearly was a tomb—there could be no doubt about that: beyond Carter's blocking lay a corridor, filled to the roof with rubble; and at the end of this a second doorway gradually revealed itself, plastered and sealed like the first. 'I asked Mr. Carter to take out a few stones and take a look in,' Lord Carnarvon was to recall a few days later:

> 'After a few minutes this was done and he pushed his head partly into the aperture. With the help of a candle he could dimly discern what was inside. A long silence followed until I said, I fear in somewhat trembling tones, "Well, what is it?" "There are some marvellous objects here" was the welcome reply! Having given up his place my daughter and myself went to the hole and I could with difficulty restrain my excitement. At first sight with the very inadequate light all one could see was what appeared to be gold bars. On getting a little more accustomed to the light it became apparent that these were colossal gilt couches with extraordinary heads, boxes here and boxes there. We enlarged the hole and Mr. Carter managed to scramble in—the chamber is sunk two feet below the bottom of the passage—

and then, as he moved about with the candle, we knew that we had found something absolutely unique and unprecedented...'[7]

After a fitful sleep, Carnarvon and Carter returned to the tomb the following day. Arthur Callender, a trusted friend of Carter who had joined the party to assist, rigged up an electric light and a more thorough investigation of the room—later dubbed the Antechamber—became possible. The far wall proved to be taken up with three large, gilded couches, piled high with boxes, chairs and other items; and beneath the first was the unblocked entrance to a second chamber—referred to by the excavators as the Annexe—filled with a disturbed, tangled mass of more funerary equipment. To the left of the couches, between two life-sized statues of the tomb owner, evidently lay a third chamber, closed off with a plastered and sealed doorway which had itself been breached and resealed in antiquity at the bottom right-hand corner.

Determined to investigate the tomb fully, on November 28th the explorers secretly breached this reblocked robbers' hole, Carter wriggling through first, followed by Carnarvon and then Lady Evelyn; Callender, too stout to insert more than his head and shoulders, remained in the Antechamber. As the excavators now discovered, here behind the wall lay the Burial Chamber, and, beyond that, a fourth room—the Treasury. But that was all. Carnarvon and Carter's new royal tomb was one of the smallest ever to have been found in the Valley.

The company returned to the Antechamber, and hid their means of access into the Burial Chamber and Treasury with the lid of a basket and some artistically arranged reeds from a decaying mat that lay conveniently to hand. The facts of the matter were now clear, and a few hours later Carnarvon was able excitedly to write to the

[7] Annotated typescript by Lord Carnarvon, December 10th, 1922, now in the Department of Egyptian Antiquities, British Museum; quoted by Reeves and Taylor, *Howard Carter Before Tutankhamun,* pp. 140-42.

Egyptologist Alan Gardiner: 'I have got Tutankamen [sic] (that is certain) and I believe ... intact'.[8]

*

[8] Letter, Carnarvon to Alan H. Gardiner, dated December 1st, 1922, in the Griffith Institute, Ashmolean Museum, Oxford; quoted by Reeves and Taylor, *Howard Carter Before Tutankhamun*, p. 142.

PHOTOGRAPH OF THE NORTHERN END OF THE ANTECHAMBER, TAKEN AFTER THE UNOFFICIAL ENTRY INTO THE BURIAL CHAMBER AND TREASURY ON THE EVENING OF NOVEMBER 28TH, 1922. THE BASKET LID AND THE REMAINS OF A REED MAT HAVE BEEN CASUALLY PROPPED UP TO CONCEAL THE EXCAVATORS' MEANS OF ACCESS—THROUGH A REBLOCKED HOLE ORIGINALLY MADE BY ROBBERS IN ANTIQUITY. [GRIFFITH INSTITUTE, OXFORD]

As the sense of wonder wore off, the awesome responsibility facing the excavators began to sink in. There was clearly much to be done, and it was obvious to Carter, the experienced professional, that emptying and documenting the tomb—whose contents were in an extremely delicate state—would take some considerable time; it would also require the skills of a number of specialists. Fortunately, the matter of staffing was quickly resolved. Because of his close relationship with the Metropolitan Museum of Art in New York, for whom he had secured a number of important pieces over the years (including the rich jewellery and other burial goods of three minor wives of Tuthmosis III),[9] Carter was able to strike a deal for the loan of two of their key Egyptian Expedition staff members—Harry Burton, their talented, Norfolk-born photographer; and Arthur C. Mace, their Associate Curator, another Englishman and the best in the business when it came to dealing with fragile materials. As the Museum surely hoped, and as Carnarvon and Carter doubtless intimated, this assistance would be fully acknowledged following a formal division of the finds. Besides these two, Carter had the foresight to bring on board a fourth Englishman, Alfred Lucas, the Egyptian Government chemist, without whose tender and informed ministrations much of what we now see on display in the Cairo Museum would have been been lost forever.

*

While Carter occupied himself with strictly archaeological matters, Lord Carnarvon looked to the business side of the discovery. Perhaps the crucial decision in this area was to channel the results of the day-to-day work exclusively through *The Times*—for an initial fee of £5,000 followed by a 75% royalty on the subsequent sale of news to other newspapers. Not only was this arrangement financially shrewd, allowing Carnarvon to recoup much of the cost of his work and more besides, but it was also intended to avoid the seri-

[9] See H. E. Winlock, *The Treasure of Three Egyptian Princesses* (New York, 1948); Thomas Hoving, *Tutankhamun. The Untold Story* (New York, 1978), esp. ch. 13.

ous disruption a large journalistic presence would have caused to the difficult task in hand. The political repercussions of this arrangement were left to others to point out, and indeed would soon make themselves felt: *The Times*'s competitors were furious, and much mischief was made as a result.

*

One of the excavators' most outspoken critics was a fellow Egyptologist of no mean ability, Arthur Weigall, who, in 1905, had succeeded Carter as Inspector-General of Antiquities for Upper Egypt. Carter, for this and other reasons, had long held a grudge against the man, and this grudge was about to be renewed: for, following the announcement of the discovery, Weigall would be taken on by the *Daily Mail* as their special correspondent at the tomb. He should have known not to expect any special favours.

The *Mail*'s correspondent was to provide a revealing insight into the characters of Lord Carnarvon and his excavator and the risks they were running. The former, he writes,

> 'is an odd mixture of Bohemian and plutocrat: a man who has seen a great deal of the underworld and is reputed to have pitted his brains against and outwitted the toughest bookies and "crooks" on the turf. He is an adventurous soul who goes his own gay way and seems to care not a jot for public opinion. His manners are notoriously bad; he is often thought to be insolent; and yet, in spite of many disadvantages he manages generally to attain his objects, and he is regarded with affection by his friends. I do not know whether he is consistently cunning, or often ingenuous'.[10]

As for Carter:

> '[He] is a man of good heart, soured by ill-health: he can be most charming, and yet is more generally thought to be

[10] Arthur Weigall, unpublished article, quoted by Julie Hankey, 'Arthur Weigall. The Tutankhamun Connection', *Minerva, The International Review of Ancient Art and Archaeology*, July/August 1994, p. 23.

> intolerably rude... He is what is called "pig-headed," and yet in spite of his blind obstinacy, he has a very charming side to his character. Neither he nor Lord Carnarvon is a scholar, but Mr. Carter is an expert field-worker, and knows as much as any man about the handling of antiquities.'[11]

'The great danger lay,' Weigall concluded, 'in the fact that both men were extremely casual and tactless, and had already aroused much native hostility, which manifested itself freely wherever servility did not veil it'.[12]

Their cavalier handling of the situation frankly appalled him, and from the very start he railed against it:

> 'You opened the tomb before you notified the government representative and, for all I know, entered it... I believe you when you tell that you respected the rights of entry, but not notifying them of the initial discovery was enough.
>
> Don't you realise that all the natives say that you may have had the opportunity to steal some of the millions of pounds' worth of gold of which you talked?'[13]

'Believe me,' Weigall continued,

> 'this is no minor situation. It is of utmost danger to Britain. You don't realise that you have created a storm of sheer hatred by two unfortunate acts: the first by slighting the government at the opening of the tomb of a Pharaoh who from nothing has come to be—in the mystical mind of the natives—a sort of omen of Nationalism, and the second, by making for money, a contract which forces you to shut out press men and Egyptologists and to behave like brigands sworn to secrecy—in fact, to the native mind, like thieves.'[14]

It was a warning the excavators would have done well to heed.

*

[11] *Ibid.*
[12] *Ibid.*
[13] Letter from Weigall to Carter, dated 25 January 1923, in the Department of Egyptian Art, Metropolitan Museum of Art, New York; quoted by Hoving, *Tutankhamun*, p. 162.
[14] Ibid.; quoted by Hoving, *Tutankhamun*, p. 164.

The official opening of the Burial Chamber took place on Sunday February 17th, 1923, in the presence of Elisabeth, Queen of the Belgians, and thirty-nine Egyptian, European and American VIPs. Slowly, carefully Carter attacked the wall with hammer and chisel, and gradually the astonishing scene which had first met the excavators' eyes eleven weeks previously was now revealed to the assem-

JAMES HENRY BREASTED (CENTRE), FOUNDING DIRECTOR OF THE ORIENTAL INSTITUTE OF THE UNIVERSITY OF CHICAGO AND A STAUNCH SUPPORTER OF CARTER, PICTURED IN THE VALLEY OF THE KINGS WITH CARTER'S FORMER RIVAL AND CURRENT OPPONENT, ARTHUR WEIGALL, NOW WORKING AS A 'SPECIAL CORRESPONDENT' FOR THE LONDON *DAILY MAIL*. [GRIFFITH INSTITUTE, OXFORD]

M E M O R A N D U M   O F   A G R E E M E N T made the ninth day of January One thousand nine hundred and twenty-three BETWEEN THE RIGHT HONOURABLE GEORGE EDWARD STANHOPE MOLYNEUX HERBERT EARL OF CARNARVON (hereinafter referred to as "the Earl") of the one part and THE TIMES PUBLISHING COMPANY LIMITED (hereinafter referred to as "the Times") of the other part WHEREAS the Earl is now conducting exploration work in the Valley of the Tomb of the Kings Luxor Egypt and has made interesting investigations which may lead to the discovery of the tomb of Tutankhamen AND WHEREAS the Earl has agreed to appoint The Times sole agents for the sale throughout the World to newspapers magazines and other publications of news articles interviews and the photographs (other than cinematograph and coloured photographs) relating thereto on the terms and conditions hereinafter contained NOW THESE PRESENTS WITNESS AND IT IS HEREBY AGREED by and between the parties hereto as follows:-

1. The Earl hereby appoints The Times as sole agents for the sale throughout the world to newspapers magazines and other publications of all news articles interviews and photographs (other than cinematograph and coloured photographs both of which are excluded from this Agreement) ...lating to the present and future exploration work conducted by the

... ants i... the T... of the Kings Luxor Egypt

ing any matter ... mbers ...

struction thereof the sam... shall be referred

the provisions of the Arbitration Act 1889.

IN WITNESS WHEREOF the Earl of Carnarvon and William Lints Smith Manager of The Times Publishing Company Limited have hereunto set their hands the day and year first above written.

(Signed) CARNARVON

(Signed) W. Lints Smith,
Manager
The Times Publishing Company Limited.

THE OPENING AND CLOSING PARAGRAPHS OF THE CONTROVERSIAL CONTRACT WITH *THE TIMES*—LORD CARNARVON'S BITTER LEGACY TO HIS ASSOCIATE, HOWARD CARTER. [HIGHCLERE CASTLE] bled audience—the outermost of Tutankhamun's huge shrines, heavily gilded and richly inlaid with blue faience. One by one, as the opening was enlarged sufficiently to allow access, the awed guests squeezed through into the Burial Chamber and into the presence of the dead king. From the gloom of the Treasury beyond, the Anubis dog, on its gilded wooden shrine, watched impassively. The VIPs, mouths agape as they stared back at this and a thousand other marvels, could scarcely believe what their eyes were seeing.

*

The tomb was closed for the season on February 26th, 1923, and the corridor and entrance refilled with rubble to keep out intruders. There was immense relief all round. The hostility of the press had been unceasing, and the political ammunition the nationalists were attempting, successfully, to make of the *Times* monopoly had put the excavators under enormous strain. There was also the nagging question of a division of the finds. At this early stage, it would seem that Carter was against a formal break-up of the assemblage, on archaeological grounds; Carnarvon, obviously, was in favour. The eventual outcome was difficult to foresee. Would the tomb be regarded as 'intact', in which case everything would pass to the Cairo Museum? Or would the evidence for robbery, despite the fact that the burial itself was undisturbed, allow Carnarvon to carry off the generous share of the treasures his contract allowed? Since 1921 Pierre Lacau, the Director of the Antiquities Service, had been lobbying to dispense altogether with the fifty-fifty division which his predecessor, Gaston Maspero, had introduced in 1884 to promote scholarly work in Egypt; in Lacau's view, times had changed and such incentives were neither justified nor desirable. If Lacau's new law were passed, the excavators' rights would be nil: they would receive what they were given—and, if Lacau had his way, that would amount to virtually nothing.

Both excavators, in short, were at the ends of their tethers—with the tomb and its treasures, with politics, and with each other.

The crunch came on February 23rd, supposedly with Carnarvon's discovery that his daughter, Lady Evelyn Herbert, had developed a crush on Carter—the hero of the hour, perhaps, but from his lordship's view a most unsuitable match. Whatever the facts of the matter, it is clear that the two men rowed bitterly, Carter finally ejecting Lord Carnarvon from his house. Despite a placatory, apologetic letter from Carnarvon, written two days later, their friendship would never be properly re-established: a little over a month later, Lord Carnarvon was dead, poisoned by an infected mosquito bite—victim, so the press claimed, of 'Pharaoh's Curse'.

*

Carter's share of 'the curse' was his associate's political legacy. With Carnarvon still alive, there had been a chance that the ever-widening cracks could be papered over; with his unexpected death, matters, in the hands of the ill-tempered Carter, would go from bad to worse.

The second season began smoothly enough. A renewal of Lord Carnarvon's concession was applied for by his widow, and Carter appointed to advise and continue with the work of clearance—all of which was fine and acceptable to the Antiquities Service. Ominously, however, the agreement with *The Times* was renewed for a second year. This was a bad move, made worse by Carter's further decision, in a clumsy attempt to deflect criticism of the newspaper's privileged position, to take on the *Times* journalist Arthur Merton as an official member of the excavating team. Carter also insisted that there should be no disruption of the work by constant streams of visitors, official or otherwise; they would be permitted to view only as and when it proved convenient.

Carter, clearly, had learned nothing from the previous season's difficulties. The outcome, documented here in exquisite detail, is history: demands, discussion, agreement, compromise, obstruction, and finally insult. Enough! Carter, mentally drained by the endless difficulties and trivial demands emanating from Morcos Hanna and the Ministry of Public Works and from Pierre Lacau and the Antiquities Service, and physically exhausted by the awesome responsibility of dismantling the fragile shrines, finally snapped. Bolstered by bad advice, on February 12th, 1924, he downed tools, leaving the heavy lid of Tutankhamun's sarcophagus suspended perilously above the king's shrouded form. It was the first strike in archaeological history, and Carter's biggest mistake.

*

Carter's precipitate action resulted in the contract for the Carnarvon concession being deemed broken, and it was duly revoked. Rather than being seen as the victim of the situation, as a selfless scholar wishing nothing more than to get on with the job, he became the villain of the piece, mindlessly putting at risk the boy-king's treasures to make his own petty point. One by one Carter's friends and supporters began to distance themselves from his high-handedness. In desperation he resorted to that bluntest of implements, the courts. And then, as an acceptable compromise was in sight, his English lawyer, F. M. Maxwell, made an ill-considered reference to the Egyptian government, now guided by the ultra-nationalist prime minister Saad Zaghlul. In the matter of the tomb of Tutankhamun, Maxwell declared, the Egyptian government had acted like bandits. The court fell silent. This was not only adding insult to injury (Maxwell, in an earlier case, had sought to have Zaghlul hanged as a terrorist), but it was deeply offensive to the Egyptians as a whole. At a time of intense, anti-British feeling in the country, it provoked rioting in the streets and complicated matters further still.

With the British Government now also baying for Carter's blood, the situation seemed irretrievable—and there were more problems to come. An official inspection of Carter's original storeroom, the tomb of Ramesses XI, had on March 30th, 1924, after Carter's departure for a lecture-tour in the United States, brought to light a wonderful and undocumented head of Tutankhamun deliberately hidden, so it appeared, in a Fortnum and Mason's wine crate. All hell broke loose: the committee clearly believed the worst—that Carter had concealed the piece intentionally, that it had, in short, been stolen from the work. Herbert Winlock, in charge of the Metropolitan Museum's Egyptian Expedition, did his best to dig Carter out—suggesting, in a coded message, that Carter might perhaps have acquired the piece for Lord Carnarvon from unofficial excavations at the site of el-Amarna in 1923. Carter rejected this alibi, stating that the head did come from the Tutankhamun tomb, and had actually been discovered in the debris of the tomb corridor. His explanation, though less than compelling, was willingly accepted by the Antiquities Service and a potential scandal averted.

*

Tutankhamun had turned rapidly from a triumph into an international incident, with English, American, French and Egyptian involvement. Carter found himself out in the cold, seemingly for good; with his back to the wall, with nothing further to lose and, as he saw it, everything to gain, he determined to set the record straight.

Tut·ankh·amen, the Politics of Discovery first appeared as a 74-page pamphlet entitled *The Tomb of Tut·ankh·amen. Statement, with Documents, as to the Events which occurred in Egypt in the Winter of 1923-24, leading to the ultimate break with the Egyptian Government [For Private Circulation only]*. It stands as Carter's apologia for the sorry mess in which he found himself, a justification of the firm stand he had taken with those—principally Pierre Lacau—whose sole, spiteful aim was to make a difficult task more difficult still. The *Statement* had been compiled prior to his lecture tour of the United States, and the first copies came off the presses in early June 1924—ironically, just as significant progress was being made on Carter's behalf by his supporters in Cairo—, in a print run of perhaps no more than a few dozen copies; the book's circulation since, because of its rarity, has been equally restricted. Despite its

THE EXCAVATION TEAM READIES ITSELF FOR A CELEBRATORY MEAL WASHED DOWN WITH FINE WINES IN THE 'LUNCHING TOMB' (KV4, EXCAVATED FOR THE 20TH DYNASTY PHARAOH RAMESSES XI), WINTER 1922-23.
THE PARTY MEMBERS COMPRISE (CLOCKWISE, LEFT TO RIGHT): THE AMERICAN EGYPTOLOGIST JAMES HENRY BREASTED, DIRECTOR OF THE ORIENTAL INSTITUTE OF THE UNIVERSITY OF CHICAGO, WHOSE BRIEF WAS TO STUDY THE HISTORICAL ASPECTS OF THE DISCOVERY; LINCOLNSHIRE-BORN HARRY BURTON, THE METROPOLITAN MUSEUM OF ART'S BRILLIANT PHOTOGRAPHER; THE ENGLISHMAN ALFRED LUCAS, CHEMIST TO THE EGYPTIAN GOVERNMENT, WHO WAS RESPONSIBLE FOR CONSERVATION; ARTHUR 'PECKY' CALLENDER, CARTER'S PRACTICAL RIGHT-HAND MAN, LATE OF THE EGYPTIAN RAILWAY SERVICE; THE TALENTED METROPOLITAN MUSEUM EGYPTOLOGIST ARTHUR C. MACE, LIKE CARTER A FORMER STUDENT OF THE GREAT FLINDERS PETRIE; HOWARD CARTER; AND THE ENGLISH EGYPTOLOGIST ALAN H. GARDINER, WHO WOULD DECIPHER THE INSCRIPTIONS FROM THE TOMB. THE PHOTOGRAPH WAS TAKEN BY LORD CARNARVON, WHOSE PLACE AT THE HEAD OF THE TABLE, SOMEWHAT PROPHETICALLY, IS EMPTY. [GRIFFITH INSTITUTE, OXFORD]

limited distribution, the unexpected appearance of the *Statement* caused a furore—and not only among Carter's enemies. Winlock, hitherto one of Carter's staunchest allies, was horrified to find himself implicated, in an appendix, in the mess of the crated Tutankhamun head, and immediately withdrew his support. Surprised by this reaction, the insensitive Carter merely shrugged and offered to remove the offending text from those copies still to be distributed. The gesture cut little ice. Other supporters were more philosophical: for James Henry Breasted, Director of the Oriental Institute at the University of Chicago and another (exasperated) supporter of Carter, if for his own political ends, 'The summary will always be a monument in the history of research in the Near East'.[15]

However, Winlock's rejection had pulled Carter up sharp; and with the intervention of Edward Robinson, Director of the Metropolitan Museum and a calming voice of reason, the troublesome Egyptologist was persuaded to suppress his controversial pamphlet altogether. He agreed also to withdraw at long last from his ill-starred confrontation with Lacau and the Egyptian Government. Carter realised that he now stood alone; he had gone as far as he could, and his anger was spent.

*

In a strangely feeble anticlimax, the problems surrounding the Tutankhamun find eventually resolved themselves. Carter agreed to renounce all personal claim to the antiquities in Tutankhamun's tomb, and Lady Carnarvon followed suit, though the Carnarvon estate refused to drop its claim to some form of compensation. A letter was duly submitted to the Egyptian Government—and elicited no response. Then, demonstrating yet again Carter's gift for poor timing, politics intervened. On November 19th, 1924, the British Commander-in-Chief of the Egyptian army, Sir Lee Stack, was assas-

[15] Copy-letter from James Henry Breasted to Carter, dated September 29th, 1924, in the Oriental Institute of the University of Chicago, OI Director's Office Corr. 1924; quoted by James, *Howard Carter*, p. 325.

sinated, resulting in the installation of a new, pro-British government. Zaghlul and the nationalists were out.

Carter, though in a stronger position now than he had been for many months, nevertheless decided to stand by his renunciation—he had simply lost the will to fight. He agreed not to renew the *Times* monopoly for a third season, and meekly accepted nominal government supervision of his work in the form of an Antiquities Service inspector, Rushdi Effendi. After the months of swagger and obstinacy, Carter had been tamed and control was once again firmly in the hands of the Egyptians.

On January 25th, 1925, Carter could at last return to the tomb to concentrate on what he did best—archaeology. Taking up where he had left off the previous year, the hazardous task of unnesting the coffins was successfully achieved; the body of the king unwrapped and revealed, in all its jewelled splendour, to an astonished world; and in due course the bulk of the treasures extracted, packed and transported, with minimal loss, to the Cairo Museum. It was a triumph. Pierre Lacau had long before recognized that the elements of Carter's character which made him such an impossible opponent—his pedantry and stubbornness—equipped him perfectly for the task in hand. If truth be told, clearing the tomb was a job no-one else wanted. Destined to take a strenuous decade of Carter's life to complete, it would ultimately be the death of him.

*

Howard Carter's *Statement* has been described as a 'dramatic act of catharsis,'[16] and indeed it reveals far more about this talented if inflexible man and his moods than many more formal documents to have come down to us. With Carter's emergence as Egyptology's most famous son, it clearly deserves wider circulation, permitting, we might hope, its all-too-human compiler a more sympathetic hearing than the politics of his time could ever have allowed.

[16] James, *Howard Carter*, p. 325.

DRAMATIS PERSONAE

(Titles—Effendi, Pasha, Dr, etc.—omitted)

Émile Baraize	*Director of Works, Egyptian Antiquities Service*
Richard Bethell	*secretary to Howard Carter*
A. H. Bradstreet	*Egypt correspondent,* New York Times *and English* Morning Post
Evaristo Breccia	*Director, Greco-Roman Museum, Alexandria*
Ahamed El-Buluk	*electrical engineer, Valley of the Kings*
Harry Burton	*photographer to the Egyptian Expedition of the Metropolitan Museum of Art, New York*
Arthur Callender	*assistant to Howard Carter*
George Edward Stanhope Molyneux Herbert, fifth Earl of Carnarvon	*sponsor of the Valley of the Kings expedition*
Almina, Countess of Carnarvon	*wife of the fifth Earl*
Howard Carter	*associate of Lord Carnarvon and discoverer of the tomb of Tutankhamun*
Mohamed Chaban/Shaaban/Shaban/Sharban	*Assistant Keeper, Cairo Museum*
Georges Daressy	*Acting Director of the Egyptian Antiquities Service, 1914-15*
Douglas Derry	*Professor of Anatomy, School of Medicine, Cairo; examined mummy of Tutankhamun*
C. C. Edgar	*Assistant Keeper, Cairo Museum (Keeper after 1923)*
Rex Engelbach	*Chief Inspector of Antiquities, Upper Egypt (Assistant Keeper, Cairo Museum after 1924)*
Fitzgerald	*uncertain*
R. A. Furness	*Residency official*
Alan Gardiner	*Egyptologist*
Ahmed Gerigar	*Carter's reis (overseer)*
Ibrahim Habib	*Antiquities Service Inspector, Luxor*
Lindsley Foote Hall	*Draughtsman to the Egyptian Expedition of the Metropolitan Museum of Art, New York*
Morcos Hanna	*Minister of Public Works*
Walter Hauser	*Architect to the Egyptian Expedition of the Metropolitan Museum of Art, New York*
Lady Evelyn Herbert	*daughter of Lord Carnarvon*
Pierre Lacau	*Director of the Antiquities Service, 1914-36*

Alfred Lucas	*Chemist to the Antiquities Service*
Albert M. Lythgoe	*Curator of Egyptian Art, Metropolitan Museum of Art, New York*
Arthur C. Mace	*Associate Curator of Egyptian Art, Metropolitan Museum of Art, New York*
Gaston Maspero	*Director of the Antiquities Service, 1881-86, 1899-1914*
F. M. Maxwell	*Carter's lawyer*
Arthur Merton	*Egypt correspondent,* The Times
'Mr. Moyne'	*representative of* The Times
Osman	*Secretary-General, Ministry of Public Works*
James Edward Quibell	*Secretary-General of the Antiquities Service*
Archibald Douglas Reid	*British surgeon*
Mohamed Riad	*Director, Legal Department, Ministry of Public Works*
Edward Robinson	*Director, Metropolitan Museum of Art, New York*
Rushdi	*Antiquities Service Inspector, Luxor*
Scott	*Residency official*
Alexander Scott	*Research chemist, British Museum*
Lee Stack	*Commander-in-Chief, Egyptian Army*
Abdel Hamid Suleman	*Minister of the Department of Public Works*
P. M. Tottenham	*Under-Secretary of State, Department of Public Works*
Arthur Weigall	*Egyptologist and special correspondent for the* Daily Mail
Herbert E. Winlock	*Assistant Director of the Egyptian Expedition of the Metropolitan Museum of Art, New York*
Antoun Youssef	*Antiquities Service official*
Mohamed Zaghlool	*Under-Secretary of State, Ministry of Public Works*
Saad Zaghlool/Zaghlul	*Egyptian Nationalist Prime Minister*

The Tomb of Tut·ankh·amen

STATEMENT

With Documents, as to the Events which occurred in Egypt in the Winter of 1923-24, leading to the ultimate break with the Egyptian Government

[*For Private Circulation only.*]

Cassell and Company, Limited
London, New York, Toronto and Melbourne

The English text reproduces faithfully that of Carter's *Statement;* the French is presented in the original language and in new translation. No attempt has been made to correct mis-spellings or inconsistencies.

The original pagination of the *Statement* is noted in the margins to facilitate reference between the two editions.

PREFATORY NOTE 1

The following pages have been prepared by Mr. Carter with a view to placing before the Scientific Societies, his friends and others interested in the Tomb of Tut·ankh·amen, a full statement of the facts which have led up to the present position with the Egyptian Government.

The relevant correspondence has been given in its entirety, and the interviews and oral negotiations have been summarized from notes made at the time, the intention being to set out the exact facts, with the addition only of such comment as may be necessary to enable the events to be followed in their proper sequence.

THE TOMB OF TUT·ANKH·AMEN 3

STATEMENT

With Documents, as to the events which occurred in Egypt in the Winter of 1923-24, leading to the ultimate break with the Egyptian Government.

The late Earl of Carnarvon, as is generally known, was deeply interested in Egyptian Archaeology, and it had been his practice for many years past to conduct, under the superintendence of Mr. Howard Carter, excavations in that country during the Winter Season.

In the year 1915 he obtained a concession from the Egyptian Government to excavate in the Valley of the Kings. This concession, as is usual in such cases, was for one year only, renewable annually, and it was still in force when, in November, 1922, the Tomb of Tut·ankh·amen was discovered.

The following is a copy of this concession:—

Ministry of Public Works
Antiquities Service

AUTHORIZATION TO EXCAVATE

I, the undersigned, Director-General of the Antiquities Service, acting in virtue of the powers delegated to me, hereby authorize the Right Honourable Earl of Carnarvon, residing at Highclere Castle, to carry out scientific excavations in the Valley of the Kings, on lands belonging to the State, free, unbuilt upon, uncultivated, not included within the Military Zone, nor comprising any cemeteries, quarries etc., and, in general, not devoted to any public use, and this on the following conditions:—

1. The work of excavation shall be carried out at the expense, risk and peril of the Earl of Carnarvon by Mr. Howard Carter; the latter should be constantly present during excavation.

2. Work shall be executed under the control of the Antiquities Service, who shall have the right not only to supervise the work, but also to alter the manner of the execution if they so deem proper for the success of the undertaking.

4 3. If a tomb, or any other monument, happens to be discovered, the Permittee or his representative is bound to give notice at once to the Chief Inspector of Upper Egypt, at Luxor.

4. To the Permittee himself shall be reserved the privilege of opening the tomb or monument discovered, and of being the first to enter therein.

5. At the moment of the opening the Chief Inspector of the Antiquities Service shall, if he considers necessary, place on the spot the number of guardians he shall deem to be required.

6. The Permittee, or his representative, after examining the said tomb or monument, and having taken such notes as he may judge necessary, shall, if so desired, hand it over to the Inspector of Antiquities Service or to any other agent to be appointed by the said Service.

7. The Permittee, or his representative, is bound to draw up forthwith a 'Procès-verbal' [written statement] showing the particularities observed at the moment of the

opening and the place occupied by each object, sub-joining thereto as many photographs and drawings as possible.

8. Mummies of the Kings, of Princes, and of High Priests, together with their coffins and sarcophagi, shall remain the property of the Antiquities Service.

9. Tombs which are discovered intact, together with all objects they may contain, shall be handed over to the Museum whole and without division.

10. In the case of tombs which have already been searched, the Antiquities Service shall, over and above the mummies and sarcophagi intended in Article 8, reserve for themselves all objects of capital importance from the point of view of history and archaeology, and shall share the remainder with the Permittee.

As it is probable that the majority of such tombs as may be discovered will fall within the category of the present article, it is agreed that the Permittee's share will sufficiently recompense him for the pains and labour of the undertaking.

11. Once the excavations are completed, the Permittee is bound to leave the site of his operations in a satisfactory condition of levelling.

12. The Permittee further engages:—

A. Not to take squeezes of coloured monuments by means of wet paper.

B. To deposit at the Museum and, if possible, at the Sultanian Library copies of such books, memoirs, pamphlets, or collections of engravings as may be published by him on the objects discovered in the course of his excavations.

C. To deliver to the Antiquities Service, within 5
two years from the day on which the works have been completed: (1) a sketch or, if necessary in the opinion

of the Service, a plan of the field of excavations, ready for publication in the Annals of the Museum; (2) a summary list referring to the plan and showing the position of the objects forming a whole, such as sarcophagi, boats, funerary statues, glassware, or amulets, etc., belonging to the same sarcophagus.

13. Any infraction, on the part of the Permittee or his agents, of the conditions above stated shall entail the cancellation of the present authorization, without any notice being given or any formality being taken.

In such case the Antiquities Service, acting departmentally, shall at once stop all work and shall take such steps as it may deem necessary in its own interests and for the safeguarding of the monuments or objects already discovered at the moment of the stoppage of the excavations, and this without the Permittee, or any agent of his, having the right to claim any indemnity or compensation whatsoever or for any reason.

The present authorization holds good for one year, to run from April 18th, 1915, subject to renewal at the discretion of the Service.

Done, in duplicate, at Cairo,
April 18th, 1915.

Acting Director-General Antiquities Service,
Signed: DARESSY.

Seen and accepted the present authorization for the Earl of Carnarvon. Signed: HOWARD CARTER

La présente autorisation est renouvelée pour une année, à partir du 16 Novembre, 1917.

Lu et approuvé. Le Caire, 12 Décembre, 1917.
(For the Earl of Carnarvon) Le Directeur Général,
Signed: HOWARD CARTER Signé: P. LACAU.

[*The present authorization is renewed for one year, from 16th November, 1917.*
Read and approved. *Cairo, 12th December, 1917.*
(For the Earl of Carnarvon) *The Director General,*
Signed: HOWARD CARTER. *Signed: P. LACAU.*]

La présente autorisation est renouvelée pour une année, à partir du 26 Novembre, 1918.
Le Caire, 26 Novembre, 1918.
Lu et approuvé. Le Directeur Général
Signed: HOWARD CARTER Signé: P. LACAU.

[*The present authorization is renewed for one year, from 26th November, 1918.*
Cairo, 26th November, 1918.
Read and approved. *The Director General*
Signed: HOWARD CARTER. *Signed: P. LACAU.*]

La présente autorisation est renouvelée pour une année, à partir du 26 Janvier, 1921.
Lu et approuvé. Le Caire, 26 Janvier, 1921.
Signed: HOWARD CARTER. (Pour le Directeur Général)
Signé: DARESSY.

[*The present authorization is renewed for one year, from 26th January, 1921.*
Read and approved. *Cairo, 26th January, 1921.*
Signed: HOWARD CARTER. *(For the Director General)*
Signed: DARESSY.]

La présente autorisation est renouvelée pour une 6
année, à partir du 16 Novembre, 1921.
Le Caire, 12 Février, 1922.
Lu et approuvé. Le Directeur Général,
Signed: HOWARD CARTER Signé: P. LACAU.

[*The present authorization is renewed for one year, from 16th November, 1921.*

Cairo, 12th February, 1922.

Read and approved. *The Director General,*
Signed: HOWARD CARTER. *Signed: P. LACAU.*]

La présente autorisation est renouvelée pour une année, à partir du 16 Novembre, 1922.

Le Caire, 15 Janvier, 1923.

Lu et approuvé, Le Directeur Général,
Signed: HOWARD CARTER. Signé: P. LACAU.

[*The present authorization is renewed for one year, from 16th November, 1922.*

Cairo, 15th January, 1923.

Read and approved. *The Director General,*
Signed: HOWARD CARTER. *Signed: P. LACAU.*]

From January to the end of March, 1923, the work in the tomb proceeded without interruption, when it was closed down for the Summer. On the 5th of April, 1923, Lord Carnarvon died in Cairo.

There had during the Winter been some friction in connexion with the supply of news, to which, under Contract with *The Times*, that newspaper was entitled to the exclusive right of publication.

After the death of the late Earl of Carnarvon, it was agreed between M. Lacau and Mr. Carter that with his death his Concession in the Valley of the Tombs of the Kings, as far as further excavation was concerned, lapsed; but that the discovery of the tomb was a *fait accompli,* and the fact that most of the objects were still in the tomb, and not yet taken out and stored in a magazine or in the Museum, was simply a matter of the correct carrying out of scientific work. The further work in the tomb, therefore, was to be regarded as *déblaiement* [clearance] and not *fouilles* [excavation].

To regularize the position, M. Lacau asked Mr. Carter to confirm this in writing, which he did as follows:—

Luxor, April 27th, 1923.

To the Director-General, Service des Antiquités, Cairo.

DEAR MONSIEUR LACAU,

In reference to our conversation regarding the completion of the work attached to the discovery of the tomb of Tut·ankh·amen, and in accordance with your wish, I beg to state formally that the family of the late Earl of Carnarvon have every desire to continue in his memory that undertaking. In other words, they wish me to represent them in that particular undertaking.

I should be glad, therefore, if you would be so kind as to put the matter in order.

Believe me, etc.,

Signed: HOWARD CARTER.

In reply Mr. Carter received the following letter and authorization:—

Service des Antiquités. Le Caire, 12 Juillet, 1923. 7

No. 27-2/6.

OBJET: DÉBLAIEMENT DE LA TOMBE DE TOUT·ANKH·AMON.

Recommandé.

Pièces jointes 2.

R.D.

MONSIEUR,—J'ai l'honneur de vous envoyer ci-joint, en double exemplaire, l'autorisation accordée à Lady Carnarvon pour achever le déblaiement de la tombe de Tout·Ankh·Amon. Je vous prie de vouloir bien faire signer cette autorisation par Lady Carnarvon et de nous la retourner ensuite.

Veuillez agréer, Monsieur, l'assurance de ma considération distinguée.

Le Directeur Général
Signé: P. LACAU

MONSIEUR H. CARTER,
Constitutional Club,
Northumberland Avenue,
London, England.
Dated: 12 Juillet, 1923.

[Antiquities Service. Cairo, 12th July, 1923.
No. 27-2/6.

OBJECT: THE CLEARANCE OF THE TOMB OF TUT·ANKH·AMON.

Registered.
Two enclosures.

SIR,–I have the honour to send you herewith, in duplicate, the authorization granted to Lady Carnarvon to complete the clearance of the tomb of Tut·Ankh·Amon. Please be so kind as to have this authorization signed by Lady Carnarvon and returned to us.

Please be assured, Sir, of my distinguished consideration.

The Director General
Signed: P. LACAU

MR. H. CARTER,
Constitutional Club,
Northumberland Avenue,
London, England.
Dated: 12th July, 1923.]

OBJET: TOMBE DE TOUT·ANKH·AMON
AUTORISATION

Lady Carnarvon est autorisée à continuer le déblaiement de la tombe de Tout·Ankh·Amon qu'elle désire achever en mémoire de Lord Carnarvon.

Le reste de la Vallée des Rois ne fait pas partie de la concession.

La présente autorisation est valable (1) pour la fin de cette saison, c'est-à-dire jusqu'au 1er novembre, 1923, et (2) pour le saison prochaine, c'est-à-dire du 1er novembre, 1923, au 1er novembre, 1924.

Elle pourra être renouvelée si le travail n'est pas terminé. Les conditions nouvelles sont identiques à celles de la concession précédente.

Le Service des Antiquités se réserve d'exercer son droit de contrôle sur le chantier de façon à éviter tous les commentaires de Presse de l'an passé et à protéger les fouilleurs dans la mesure du possible contre les visites inutiles.

Il va sans dire que le droit de publication est réservé entièrement, suivant l'usage, à Lady Carnarvon.

C'est Mr. Carter qui dirigera le chantier et qui représentera sur place Lady Carnarvon.

Signé: Le Directeur Général
Du Service des Antiquités

Lu et approuvé. P. LACAU

Signed: ALMINA CARNARVON.

[*OBJECT: THE TOMB OF TUT·ANKH·AMON*
AUTHORIZATION

Lady Carnarvon is authorized to continue the clearance of the tomb of Tut·ankh·Amon which she wishes to complete in memory of Lord Carnarvon.

The rest of the Valley of the Kings does not form part of this concession.

The present authorization is valid (1) for the remainder of this season, that is, to the 1st November, 1923, and (2) for the following season, that is from the 1st November, 1923 to the 1st November, 1924.

> *It may be renewed if the work is not completed. The new conditions are identical to those of the previous concession.*
>
> *The Antiquities Service reserves the right of control over the site so as to avoid comment such as that in the Press last year and to protect the team as far as possible from needless visits.*
>
> *It goes without saying that publication rights are reserved entirely, as is customary, to Lady Carnarvon.*
>
> *Mr Carter will direct the works and will represent Lady Carnarvon on the site.*
>
> *Signed: the Director General*
> *of the Antiquities Service*
> *Read and approved. P. LACAU.*
> *Signed: ALMINA CARNARVON*]

By these documents it will be seen at once that Almina
Countess of Carnarvon was authorized to continue the
déblaiement [clearance] of the tomb, in the memory of Lord
Carnarvon, up to November 1st, 1924; that she could renew the
authorization if the work was not then terminated; that the condi-
8 tions of the work were identical with those of the original concession; that the Antiquities Service reserved itself the right of control
in matters connected with the Press, in order to avoid commen-
taries such as occurred during the preceding season, and agreed to
protect Mr. Carter against *visites inutiles* [needless visits]; that the
right of publication was reserved entirely to Almina Countess of
Carnarvon; and, finally, that it was to be Mr. Carter who was to
be in charge of the work, and to represent Almina Countess of
Carnarvon therein.

Mr. Carter arrived in Cairo on October 8th, 1923.

On October 11th he conferred with Mr. Quibell, the Secretary-General of the Antiquities Service, in M. Lacau's absence acting Head of the Department in the Cairo Museum, with regard to the official arrangements for the coming season's campaign. In this interview the question was discussed as to the best measures to be taken to avoid:—

1. Newspaper disputes.
2. Difficulties with regard to visitors.

Both of which had caused friction with the Antiquities Service during the preceding season.

A record of this interview is given in the following memorandum:

NOTE ON CONVERSATION WITH
MR. HOWARD CARTER, OCTOBER 11TH, 1923.

Mr. Carter and I discussed to-day what measures should be taken to avoid the newspaper disputes and the difficulties about visitors which, last year, rendered the Tutankhamen work so difficult.

I had two propositions: (1) the giving of a short daily bulletin to the Press Bureau, and (2) the opening of the tomb once a week to a limited number of visitors by dated and numbered tickets issued by the Public Works Ministry.

Mr. Carter, who has necessarily given much more time and consideration to the problem than I could, made the following propositions which, in some respects, offer a better and simpler solution:

(1) THE PRESS.—He has taken on his staff Mr. Merton, last year *The Times* correspondent, and proposes to give through him the same daily report to *The Times* and to the Egyptian Press. *The Times* news would be cabled out in the evening, to be printed in the next day's paper. The same news would be given to the Egyptian Press early in the morning, in ample time to be printed in the papers of the day. Thus the news would reach the public in London and in Cairo practically at the same time.

This is, I must say, a generous offer. The Cairo newspapers will get for nothing what all European and American papers will have to pay for.

(2) VISITORS.—Mr. Carter pointed out that to admit visitors one day each week involves a very serious loss of time. The day before visitors are received, all delicate objects must be removed or especially protected; tools must be put away; electric wiring altered, and a clear path made. All this involves hours of work the day before, and hours of work the day after. One whole day and parts of two other days are sacrificed.

9 He proposes that no visitors should enter until a definite part of the work is done—the removal, for example, of one of the big shrines—and that then the work [be] interrupted, for a week if necessary, while parties of visitors pass through. They should be admitted by tickets obtained at the Public Works Ministry. He points out with perfect truth that there will be little to see for the most of this year. The two small chambers must be left for safety boarded and bricked up; the great shrines will have to be taken to pieces plank by plank, covered with cloth and lashed to keep the ornament in place, and brought out one by one to the Laboratory tomb. Working on these large timbers in a confined space, the workers will need the suppleness of weasels to creep in and out themselves, and for many a day it will be materially impossible for a stout man or an oldish man or lady to get into the tomb at all.

We may expect that the dullness of the spectacle as seen from the door will soon be realized, and that we shall not have the crowd of would-be visitors that were so embarrassing last year.

[The account of my propositions is accurate.—Signed: HOWARD CARTER.]

I think this plan is worth trying, and should be tried, but we should not lose sight of the possibility that it might not work, and that we should have to ask Mr. Carter to modify it and to admit selected visitors every fortnight or every week. But every day lost through showing visitors

AN EGYPTIAN GOVERNMENT DELEGATION PHOTOGRAPHED AT THE ENTRANCE TO THE EXPEDITION'S AD HOC 'LABORATORY' IN THE TOMB OF SETHOS II (KV15). A SMILING CARTER OCCUPIES CENTRE STAGE; BEFORE HIM STANDS HIS NEMESIS, THE BEARDED JESUIT PIERRE LACAU, FRENCH DIRECTOR OF THE EGYPTIAN ANTIQUITIES SERVICE. [GRIFFITH INSTITUTE, OXFORD]

round has to be paid for by a day or more of the abominable heat of the month of May, and I sincerely hope the arrangement may work satisfactorily.

The first proposition is manifestly acceptable; it offers much more than the Cairo papers can expect, or would indeed ask for.

Signed: J. E. QUIBELL.

It will be seen that Mr. Quibell was in absolute agreement with Mr. Carter's proposals with regard to Press matters, and also with regard to the question of visits, though on this latter point he thought some modification might later prove necessary.

On October 12th Mr. Carter made a special trip to Alexandria to see His Excellency Abdel Hamid Pasha Suleman, the Minister of the Department of Public Works, and submitted the programme already discussed with Mr. Quibell.

In the conversation that took place Mr. Carter pointed out to His Excellency that it would be better both for the work and in the general interest that, over and above the programme stated above, visits should not be allowed until a definite part of the season's work had been carried out. That then, after an official inspection or opening, and after the scientific records had been made, visitors should be allowed to enter by tickets obtained through the Ministry of Public Works for such period (a week or more) as should be considered necessary. This occasion would probably present itself after the opening of the Sarcophagus. The other two chambers—so-called Annexe and Store Chamber [Treasury]—would temporarily be closed until the moment for dealing with them should come. His Excellency was sympathetic to this plan, and asked Mr. Carter to submit it to the Residency, stating that if they (the Residency) agreed to it he also would agree. This Mr. Carter did the same morning, and the Residency concurred.

The following note will be of interest in this connexion:

The Residency, Ramleh 10
Oct. 17th, 1923

DEAR HOWARD CARTER,

I return, with many thanks, the note you left with me. I have shown it to Scott, who remarked that he feared the proposals about visitors would cause disappointment to many tourists.

Yours sincerely,
Signed: R. A. FURNESS.

On October 16th Mr. Carter left Cairo for Luxor, accompanied by Mr. Callender and Mr. Burton.

On October 18th he crossed to Gurna and inspected the tomb, the Laboratory [tomb of Sethos II, KV15] and the Magazine [tomb of Ramesses XI, KV4], all of which he found in perfect order, thanks to the vigilance exercised by his Egyptian staff. He made arrangements with his men to commence preliminary operations on the Monday following (October 22nd).

By October 28th the tomb was once more laid bare as far as the top of the staircase, and masons had begun repairing and putting in order the retaining walls.

As the following document shows, the beginning of the work was in danger of being hampered by the question of certain formalities with regard to the light, even though the Department was aware that Mr. Carter was commencing operations at an early date. The Department was not supplying light for *public* use until November 15th.

Service des Antiquités
Inspectorat de la Haute Egypt.
Luxor, 28 Octobre, 1923.

MY DEAR CARTER,

I have sent your letter on to Quibell. What has

happened is that after all these years the Department insists that the job as *Osta* to the Crossley shall be put up to auction in Luxor.

There is naturally no one who will undertake the work except Ahamed El-Buluk. I have urged the importance of taking him on at a reasonable figure, and ought to hear to-morrow. If I don't hear before the first of November I will make temporary arrangements with him so as not to let you lose time. I shall be over at Qurneh the day after to-morrow. If there is anything you want me for at the Tombs of the Kings, I can come over.

Kindest regards, yours,

Signed: REX ENGELBACH.

To overcome any difficulty that might arise from departmental reasons, Mr. Carter, as he had done in the previous season, offered to cover any expense.

On October 29th Mr. Carter received a letter from Mr. Quibell, reading as follows:—

28th October, 1923, Heluan.

DEAR CARTER,

I see that we shall have to unpack some more of the Tout [Tutankhamun] stuff before the tourists come. I ought to have foreseen this.

11 Six more cases, all of the same size, are now nearing completion. I suppose another 20 days will see them put up. Now, would you like anyone of your team to help us in this job, if anyone be free?

Is there any particular object that you would like shown, or any that you would specially like to have kept back till you can give a hand with the unpacking ?

Bradstreet came to see me yesterday. He was going to

see the Minister afterwards. As I am to have an interview with Abdel Hamid Pasha to-morrow about other matters, he may speak about the journalists too.

Yours always,

Signed: J. E. QUIBELL.

On October 31st Mr. Carter received a letter from Mr. Quibell. In this Mr. Quibell warns him that certain British news-

HORDES OF SIGHTSEERS AT THE ENTRANCE TO THE TOMB OF TUTANKHAMUN. ARTHUR MACE OF THE METROPOLITAN MUSEUM OF ART, STANDING AT THE ENTRANCE WEARING A WHITE SUN-HELMET, SUPERVISES THE REMOVAL OF A MODERN CRATE CONTAINING FUNERARY OBJECTS CLEARED FROM THE ANTECHAMBER. [GRIFFITH INSTITUTE, OXFORD]

paper correspondents had been to see him and were threatening to make trouble. He also mentioned that the Government wanted to place Egyptian inspectors to exercise surveillance over his work, and that he would shortly be writing him officially on the subject. With this letter he enclosed a rough memorandum made by Mr. Tottenham, the Under-Secretary of the Department of Public Works, as a result of a conversation which he had with Mr. Bradstreet with regard to the Press arrangements in the tomb. Mr. Bradstreet in this conversation had made the demand that a communiqué should be issued to the Press generally not later than 9 P.M. of the same day on which *The Times* message was sent, stating that, though this would be too late for the evening papers in England, it would be in time for the morning papers of the following day. He added that if this were done there would be peace, whereas otherwise the foreign Press would take steps to get the information. At the same time he had raised an objection to the fact that Mr. Merton had been placed on Mr. Carter's staff.

In Mr. Tottenham's memorandum an emphatic statement is made that leakage of news must be prevented, and that everything possible should be done to safeguard Mr. Carter's arrangement with *The Times*. In spite of this the suggestion is made that a bulletin be issued to the Press Bureau at 8 P.M. daily by the Antiquities Service, in order that agents of papers not in alliance with *The Times* might be enabled to forward their news in time for publication in the morning papers of the following day.

Obviously, if this proposal were carried into effect, *The Times* contract would fall to the ground; and the memorandum ends by asking Mr. Quibell to write to Mr. Carter to explain the difficulties, and to ask his view as to how best they could be met.

In this connexion it may be stated that Mr. Carter had already pointed out to His Excellency the Minister and to Mr. Quibell that the question of *The Times* contract, which was the chief bone of contention, was a legacy which he, as agent to the estate of the late

Earl of Carnarvon, was bound to carry out, whatever his own personal feelings in the matter might be.

Following the confidential letter, Mr. Carter received on November 1st the following document:—

31st October, 1923. 12
Museum, Cairo.

DEAR CARTER,

I have seen Tottenham again this morning, and he feels, and I agree with him, that we ought to see you again before making final arrangements about the bulletin, about 'surveillance,' and so on.

Inshallah, we can make an agreement—once for all—and avoid disputes and the miseries of last year.

So we propose to come to Luxor by the night train on Monday, and to be at Luxor on Tuesday, the 6th. Will you arrange to meet us there? We shall go back the same night. Lacau comes on the 3rd, and if he likes to come with T— instead of me, of course it's for him to say. But I think he will have more than enough to occupy him here, and will be glad to send me. Winlock has arrived. No sign of Mace.

Yours sincerely,

Signed: J. E. QUIBELL.

P.S.—I rather expect you may have to come down later to see the Minister, perhaps about the 8th. I can't be sure, but it is as well you should know, as this may influence your programme of work.

Signed: J. E. Q.

To this Mr. Carter replied by wire that he would come to Cairo, and would meet Mr. Tottenham and Mr. Quibell there on November 4th. Personally he felt that this reopening of the question was somewhat unnecessary, for he had already submitted to the authorities, in

Cairo and Alexandria, what he considered a perfectly fair programme, and one which they expressed themselves quite ready to accept. Moreover, he had warned the Minister in Alexandria that there were sure to be attacks by the opposition Press, and had pointed out to Mr. Quibell, to the Minister, and to all concerned that, with two exceptions—the *Ahram* and the *Egyptian Mail*—the Egyptian newspapers had accepted the news service.

On November 4th Mr. Carter arrived at the Ministry at 10.30 A.M., and, in Mr. Tottenham's office, met Mr. Tottenham himself, M. Lacau, the Director General of the Antiquities Service —who had only returned from leave the previous day, and had thus taken no part in the previous negotiations —and Mr. Quibell. He immediately became aware that there was a change in the general atmosphere, for he found that the Government representatives had armed themselves with legal advice, and were persisting, moreover, in maintaining an alleged right of the Government to issue a daily bulletin at 8 P.M. This 'publicity right', as they termed it, was something quite new and unheard-of, and had not a single word of documentary evidence to support it.

Mr. Carter pointed out at once that this evening bulletin would involve the breaking, not only of the original *Times* contract, but also of the sub contracts made by *The Times* with the world's Press. For that reason, and in consideration of the benefits which the Government was deriving from the late Earl of Carnarvon's work in the Valley of the Kings, Mr. Carter asked, as a special favour, that the Government should waive its alleged right, and should allow him to carry out his programme, a programme which up to the present moment they had been in sympathy with.

A long discussion ensued, but finally an agreement was
13 reached, subject, of course, to confirmation of the Minister. In this the Government waived its alleged right to issue summary bulletins, and confided all 'duties of publication' to Mr. Carter. At the

same time, details regarding visits to the tomb and surveillance over the work, regarding which there was no real difference of opinion, were likewise agreed upon. The following memorandum was then drawn up and presented to the Minister, who, after reading it through twice, expressed his assent:—

> [*Memorandum*]
>
> 1. It was proposed that, in consideration of the services rendered by the late Lord Carnarvon and his agents, in order to put a stop to journalistic disputes and to facilitate the work, the Government, as an exceptional case, should waive its rights to issue summary bulletins and should confide all the duties of publication to the diggers.
>
> 2. It was proposed that an Egyptian representative of the Antiquities Department should always be present and oversee the investigations. Mohamed Eff. Sharban, Assistant Keeper of the Museum, would carry out this work better than anyone else of whom we can think.
>
> 3. *Visits.*—When the removal of the great shrines has so far progressed that it becomes materially practicable for strangers to be admitted, the work will be interrupted for a week or more, and a certain number of visitors, furnished with numbered and dated tickets obtained from the ministry of Public Works, will be admitted. This will probably be in January.

The Minister then asked Mr. Carter whether he would, out of courtesy, agree to his inviting 'one representative of the Press *per diem* to the tomb'. Mr. Carter replied that he would be agreeable to this, providing the visit took place between the hours of 10 and 11 A.M. 'Very well', said the Minister, turning to Mr. Tottenham, 'I will look after the Egyptian press, and you will look after the foreign press.' Mr. Tottenham demurred, and as he, M. Lacau, and

Mr. Quibell were evidently not in sympathy with the proposal, Mr. Carter made the following suggestion. In order that no loophole should be left on either side, he proposed that all the parties concerned should give this particular matter twenty-four hours' consideration, and that then they should meet and compare their views.

Mr. Carter's own decision is shown in the following memorandum, which he took with him to the Ministry on the following morning (November 5th):—

> [*Memorandum*]
>
> REPRESENTATIVES OF EUROPEAN PRESS IN REGARD TO VISITING TOMB
>
> I see no objection to this proposal, provided that: No one individual representative is given more than one permit (say) per fourteen days, no matter how many papers he represents, and that visit be between 10 and 11 in the morning. I ask in the interests of the work in general—which is the Government interest—that not more than one Press representative is authorised to visit the tomb per day.
>
> I undertake on my side to facilitate these visits to the best of my ability. H .C.

14 To his surprise, this question of a daily Press visit was entirely ignored, and he found that Mr. Tottenham, M. Lacau, and Mr. Quibell were insisting upon a complete reopening of the whole question. As a result, matters which had been agreed upon and settled on the previous day were again brought into discussion, a discussion which continued in a vicious circle, and the question of one daily Press visit, which was to have been the subject of the interview, was never even presented to the Minister.

After a great deal of fruitless argument the following question was put to Mr. Carter:—

[*Memorandum* (written by Mr. Tottenham)]

Why is it in the best interests of the Government to waive its rights to issue information, to confide that issue to heirs of Lord Carnarvon, and to refuse to give even a brief daily bulletin to the world at large?

And Mr. Tottenham asked him to give as strong an answer as possible, so that he could quote it as adequate justification of the Government's action.

Mr. Carter then prepared a statement (herewith quoted), which he presented to Mr. Tottenham on November 6th.

[*Memorandum*]

QUESTION PUT FORWARD BY THE UNDER SECRETARY OF STATE FOR P.W.D.

Q. Why is it in the best interests of the Gov. to waive its rights to issue information, to confide that issue to the heirs of Lord Carnarvon, and to refuse to give even a brief daily bulletin to the world at large?

Reply.—The following remarks are respectfully submitted in reply to the above question; but, having regard to the form in which the question is framed, it is felt necessary to state that the reply must be regarded, in lawyers' language, as 'without prejudice' (sous les plus amples réserves).

The contract with *The Times* was made to protect ourselves from the importunities of Press correspondents, by enabling us to deal with one organization for world distribution, instead of a large number of individual Press representatives, which would have entailed a great loss of time and interference with the research work.

This contract, accepted by the large majority of the world's Press, excited opposition on the part of certain papers, which had and indeed still have, opportunity of taking the service, but which for purely personal reasons refused it.

Since last year the number of sub-contracts made with *The Times* by the world's Press has increased, and newspapers which had been in opposition last season have accepted *The Times* service this year.

The reliability and efficiency of this service have never, to our knowledge, been called into question.

Moreover, the contract was made in good faith, solely with the object of ensuring that the work, on the delicate nature of which it is unnecessary to insist, be carried on with the minimum of interruption and friction. It can scarcely be necessary to dwell on the importance of working, so far as possible, on a regular system calculated to ensure this result.

The proceeds of the contract are entirely devoted to research work at the tomb, and are thus wholly for the benefit of science, of Egypt and of the Egyptian Government; whereas the sole object of the opposition is to secure material benefit for themselves.

It is therefore obviously in the interest of science, and consequently should also be in that of the Eg. Gov., that the agent should be protected in the matter of this contract.

Last year, in our desire to meet the wishes of the Gov., we agreed to allow weekly visits from newspaper correspondents. So far from this concession producing peace, it is a fact that the attacks and insults directed against Lord Carnarvon and the members of his staff became more virulent and continued till his Lordship's last breath.

It is for these reasons that I beg the Eg. Gov. to protect me, acting as agent, in every possible way.

The only way in which I can be protected is by the

Gov. not issuing the proposed communiqués, but relying on me to communicate all information to the world through the medium of the service already instituted.

Naturally this may cause jealousy on the part of the opposition, who will thus not be able to derive the material benefits they want. With firmness, however, such opposition can be frustrated, and the interests of science will undoubtedly be furthered thereby.

In other words, by carrying out your proposal of even a brief daily bulletin you would be aiding a private enterprise and thus acting against the interests of science.

Mr. Tottenham objected that this was not sufficiently strongly worded to stifle criticism, and asked him to prepare a more emphatic statement.

[*Revised Memorandum*]

REPLY TO QUESTION PUT FORWARD BY THE UNDER-SECRETARY OF STATE, P.W.D.

The following remarks are submitted in reply to the above question; but, having regard to the form in which the question is framed, it is felt necessary to state that the reply must be regarded, in lawyers' language, as 'without prejudice' (sous les plus amples réserves).

The contract with *The Times* was made to protect ourselves from the importunities of Press correspondents, by enabling us to deal with one organization for world distribution instead of a large number of individual Press representatives, which would otherwise have entailed a great loss of time and interference with the research work.

It was made in good faith, solely with the object of ensuring that the work, on the delicate nature of which it is unnecessary to insist, be carried out with the minimum

of interruption and friction. It can scarcely be necessary to
dwell on the importance of working, so far as possible, on
a regular system calculated to ensure this result. In no part
16 of the concession is there anything which would lead the
concessionnaire to believe that he was not within his
rights in making such an arrangement.

The contract with *The Times*, accepted by the large majority of the world's Press and approved by scientific authorities, has excited opposition on the part of certain papers, which had, and indeed still have, the opportunity of taking the service, but which for purely personal reasons they still refuse.

Since last year the number of sub-contracts made with *The Times* by the world's Press has increased, and newspapers which had up to then been in opposition have accepted *The Times* service this year.

It may be most emphatically pointed out that in the agreement it is definitely laid down that there shall be no preference in treatment of any individual paper taking the service, and that the Egyptian Press shall receive the same service free of all charge.

The result is that, in fact, official information as to the progress of the research work is enabled to be published daily, by all papers contracting with *The Times*, at one and the same time.

The proceeds of the contract are entirely devoted to research work at the tomb, and are thus wholly for the benefit of science, of Egypt and the Egyptian Government. On the other hand, the opposition are entirely self-actuated, their sole object being to break the arrangement of the service and to secure material benefit for themselves.

The issue of even a brief daily bulletin is not only unnecessary but would also be seriously prejudicial to the service; it would decrease the value of the material I am supplying under my agreement; and in acceding to pressure from the opposition in this respect the Government would at once become the supporter of a venture for purely private benefit and would be acting against the interest of science, since the proceeds of my arrangement are, as mentioned, devoted to research work.

Further, such an issue as the Government proposes would immediately produce graver trouble, not only with *The Times*, but also with all the sub-contractors—namely, the papers all the world over taking the service. It would involve a gigantic lawsuit on the score of breach of contract, into which the Government would be most infallibly drawn. It would also mean the absolute interruption and suspension of the whole work for an indefinite period.

You have represented to me, though I am not of that opinion, that only scientific publication is my property and that publicity is the Government right. I repeat that there is nothing in the concession to this effect. Neither is there any law existing to cover this case, and such a question could only be proved by legal proceedings, which I should certainly feel myself obliged to take should the Government decide to enforce its alleged rights.

The question of the right of publicity is therefore, in these circumstances, merely a matter of opinion. One would have expected that in such a case the Government would have given the benefit of the doubt to its concessionnaire. Instead of this, it is taking the part of those who throughout have tried to do him harm, who have only a material interest in the matter, and who are seeking to intimidate the Government into giving them, as a concession for personal profit, what they could have secured 17
without fuss if they had only cared to come into line with

the rest of the world's Press and accept a service conducted solely for the benefit of scientific research.

Again, if the Government says that only scientific right of publication is my property, then why is it, and how is it, that it allows that right to be infringed in this country? At the Government's own request we invited its representatives to see the discovery. *Bulletin de la Société Archéologique d'Alexandrie,* No. 19, par. Ev. Breccia, 'Le Tombeau de Tutankhamon,' shows how advantage is taken of our benevolence. It is a striking example of how the Government treats sacred rights, of how little it protects such right.

Further, last year, in our desire to meet the wishes of the Government, we agreed to allow weekly visits from newspaper correspondents. So far from this concession producing peace, it resulted in the attacks and insults directed against Lord Carnarvon and the members of his staff becoming more virulent and continuing to this day.

Again, we acceded to the Government's wish for the instalment of a representative in the Valley. This not only proved an utter failure, but also ended in serious breach of faith. If the Government enforces what it considers to be its rights it will be incurring grave responsibility and grave consequences; and although I am, and wish to continue, its friend, I shall be forced to take up the cudgels against it.

To protect myself against any such action as the Government might contemplate, I should feel compelled to defend by all possible means myself and the interests which I represent as agent of the late Lord Carnarvon's heirs.

May I just say that such a state of things would be a poor recompense for the services I have rendered to the Egyptian Government.

This would involve making known to the world in the

fullest detail the whole of our negotiations from start to finish. The action of the Government, the action of the opposition, and my own action would be clearly revealed, and the world would learn with amazement and disgust of the utter inadequacy of the protection which the Government affords its concessionnaires, of its lack of consideration for those working for scientific interests, and of the persistent encouragement which it is giving to the section of the Press which last year earned the lively reprobation of the thinking world by the abominable manner in which it attacked this agreement for its own ends.

For all these reasons it is obviously in the interest of the Egyptian Government that the agent should be protected in the matter of this contract. The only way in which he can be protected is by the Government not issuing the proposed communiqué, but relying on him to communicate all information to the world through the medium of the service already instituted.

I sincerely trust that the above will convince the Government of the direction in which their best interests lie. I have endeavoured throughout to be conciliatory, and no one desires a peaceful settlement more than I do. But, if the Government persists in its intention, I feel bound to say quite frankly that I shall be compelled to take action against it in the manner indicated, for in this matter I am defending not only the interests of my principals, but also *18*
those of the entire scientific world.

If the Government should be in doubt about my statements, I earnestly urge it, in its own interest, before taking action either way, to inquire what the unanimous opinion in the thinking world is with regard to this dispute and to the action of the opposition.

In conclusion, and by the way of summarizing my remarks, I would point out:—

1. There is no necessity and no justification whatever either in the interest of science or of the public for establishing an additional news service. The information now given is official—that is to say, it is supplied by the excavator himself—and every paper can, and most papers do, obtain and publish that information at one and the same time by arrangement with *The Times*.

2. It cannot be too strongly emphasized that the arrangement with *The Times* was entered into in the interests of the work itself. That work being of the most delicate character, it became essential to organize a news service on a regular system. The system adopted was that there should be only one—and that the official—channel of information. In this respect the interest of the Government is surely the same as that of the concessionnaire—namely, a regular official supply of news, involving the minimum of friction and interference with the work and ensuring to the public none but authentic information.

3. Whether or no the Government are entitled to claim the publicity rights in this case is a legal question which only the Courts can decide.

4. What is now proposed would, in fact, amount to an interference with the existing contract, or rather existing contracts, entered into in good faith, and operating to the advantage of science and without detriment of any kind to the public or Press.

5. In the case of Government excavations the Government would naturally be within its rights to supply the Press with information. But in the case of private excavations, carried out with non-Government funds, the Government has not the right to take from the conces-

sionnaire the results of his work and distribute them promiscuously for sale in the streets.

The foregoing memorandum was therefore submitted by Mr. Carter to Mr. Tottenham, M. Lacau, and Mr. Quibell on November 7th at 6 P.M., Messrs. Fitzgerald and Merton being also present. Mr. Tottenham was quite satisfied with the statement and appended to it the following note:—

> [*Memorandum* (by TOTTENHAM, in his own handwriting)]
>
> If issue of bulletin means trouble for Carter with *The Times*, and consequent interruption of work, this is a valid argument for Carter's case.

But Mr. Tottenham was unable to get M. Lacau and Mr. Quibell to express a definite opinion either way.

An endless discussion followed, in which the whole question
was again reopened from the very beginning, until finally at 8.30
P.M. Mr. Carter withdrew, suggesting that the Government repre- 19
sentatives would be more likely to reach a decision if they were left
to discuss the matter in private. At about noon on the following
morning (November 8th), in reply to a telephone message from
Mr. Carter, Mr. Tottenham informed him that the Government
were in practical agreement, and this naturally led Mr. Carter to
believe that the matter was settled and that he would be free to
return to Luxor.

In a second telephone conversation, a day or two later, Mr. Carter was promised that a covering document would be ready for him to sign on Saturday (November 10th).

On Sunday morning (November 11th), not having received this document, nor any further news from the Ministry, Mr. Carter made further inquiries, and found that the Department was again shilly-shallying, and had only a vague promise of some definite settlement on the following Tuesday (November 13th). Eight days had now been wasted in Cairo in fruitless negotiations, and, owing to the exigencies of the work, Mr. Carter was unable to delay his return to Luxor any further. Wishing, however, to arrive at something definite before he left, he got into telephone communication with the Minister, and was assured that everything would be settled satisfactorily. He accordingly left for Luxor on the night of the 11th. Mr. Mace arrived in Cairo on the 12th, and with Mr. Bethell left for Luxor on the 13th, bringing with him the Government's decision, which ran as follows:—

MINISTRY OF PUBLIC WORKS

C2 OBJECT: TUT·ANKH·AMEN'S TOMB

HOWARD CARTER, ESQ. Cairo, 13.11.1923

SIR,—With reference to recent conversations upon the subject of the measures to be taken by the Egyptian Government in relation to this season's work on the Tomb of Tut·ankh·amen, I have the honour to inform you that the following measures are proposed:—

1. The Antiquities Department shall always be represented at the Tomb to oversee the operations. The Inspector-in-Chief at Luxor and three Egyptian officials of the Department will be named for this duty.

2. The Press Bureau will issue regularly in Cairo, early in the morning, reports about the operations of the previous day.

3. Representatives of the Press, not exceeding fifteen in number, furnished with numbered and dated tickets obtained from the Public Works Ministry, will be admitted once a fortnight.

4. When the removal of the great shrines has so far progressed that it becomes materially practicable for

strangers to enter, work shall be interrupted for a week or more and a certain number of visitors (again with numbered and dated tickets from the Ministry of Public Works) shall be admitted.

It is understood that you will give to the Press Bureau,

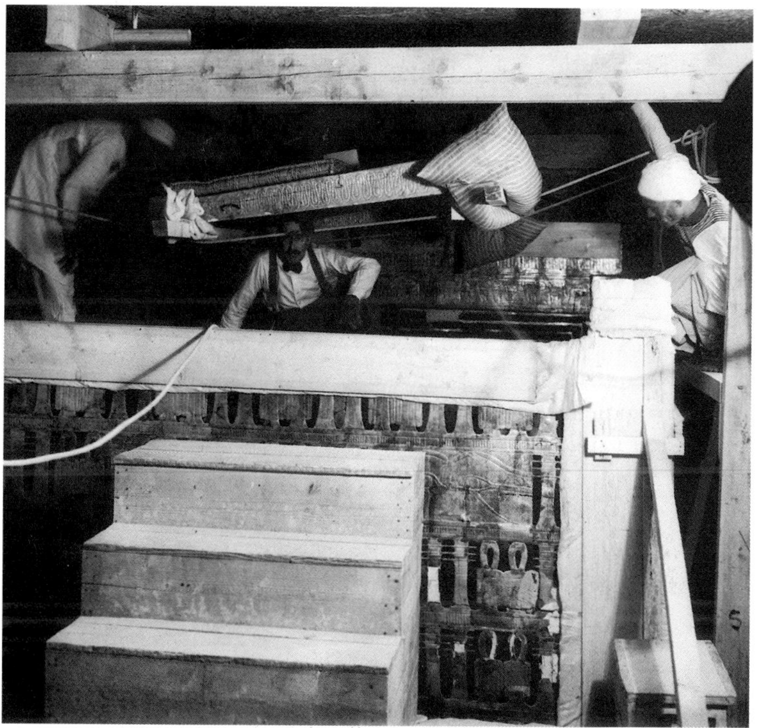

HOWARD CARTER SUPERVISES HIS TWO CHIEF WORKMEN IN THE DISMANTLING OF TUTANKHAMUN'S HUGE SHRINES OF GILDED WOOD. THE OUTERMOST SHRINE OCCUPIED PRACTICALLY THE WHOLE OF THE BURIAL CHAMBER; WITHIN IT WERE NESTED A WOODEN FRAME SUPPORTING A FRAGILE, SEQUINED PALL, A FURTHER THREE SHRINES, AND THE QUARTZITE SARCOPHAGUS WITH ITS ANTHROPOID COFFINS OF GILDED WOOD. THE SECOND OF THESE CONTAINED A THIRD COFFIN, OF SOLID GOLD, AND THE MASKED AND HEAVILY BEJEWELLED MUMMY OF TUTANKHAMUN HIMSELF.
[GRIFFITH INSTITUTE, OXFORD]

for issue to the Press of Egypt, the same daily report as is sent to *The Times*, in ample time to permit of its being printed in the papers of the day, so that, as you have suggested, the same news will reach the public in London and Cairo practically at the same time.

It may be found expedient, in addition to admitting visitors under the above regulations, to issue permits for casual visits to persons of note. It is understood that these will be restricted to the absolute minimum.

This decision has been arrived at after very careful consideration, and it is hoped and believed that the measures proposed will prove satisfactory. It must, however, be clearly understood that these measures necessarily cannot be of more than a temporary nature. Whether or not they will be maintained, wholly or partially, during the season must essentially depend upon the results realized. The Government will consequently reserve the absolute discretion to withdraw them in whole or in part, and to substitute therefore new regulations. The issue of these or other regulations is without prejudice to the terms of the concession.

Your attention is expressly called to the fact that by issuing these or other regulations in addition to or substitution for them, the Government will not in any way waive or surrender any of its rights or claims whatsoever, and in particular will maintain its absolute right, which it has hitherto maintained and in its discretion exercised, of publishing at such a time or times as it shall think fit, in the form of a periodical bulletin or otherwise, all information concerning the Tomb and the operations in connexion therewith, not amounting to information of a purely scientific nature, the publication of which by usage is ceded to diggers.

The hope is expressed that the proposed measures will result in the smooth working both of the operations under your charge and of the various services of the State directly or indirectly concerned; their success must, to a very large extent, depend upon the sympathetic and tactful co-operation of yourself and your staff, for which the Ministry will look to you with confidence.

This Department, actuated by desire to facilitate in every way possible your difficult task, will, in carrying these rules into effect, do its best to adhere to them both in their spirit and, so far as possible, in detail; but it must further be clearly understood that a rigid adherence to any rules of this nature might lead to just those difficulties which it is desired most earnestly to avoid, and with which experience has already familiarized you. For instance, it is intended to restrict the number of journalists permitted at any one time to visit the Tomb to fifteen, but this Ministry will reserve an absolute discretion to increase that number in case circumstances shall indicate a necessity. It will, in so doing, take into consideration the exigencies of your operations, and will look to you at the same time for a reciprocal consideration.

I trust that I may expect a reply from you very shortly, expressing your agreement to the above measures, in order that I may be in a position to submit them without delay to His Excellency the Minister, with a view to obtaining his approval.

I have the honour to be, Sir,
Your obedient Servant,
Signed: J. E. QUIBELL,
For Director-General Antiquities Department.

It will be recognized that this document, though acceptable on *21* the main points, was, as a contract, rendered practically useless by reservations under which the whole question could be brought up for discussion again at any moment. Mr. Carter's colleagues had already presented this view of the case to Mr. Tottenham, and it was agreed with him that, to protect Mr. Carter's interests, and to prevent the arrangement from being entirely one-sided, the following form of acceptance of the Government's proposals would be in order.

Continental-Savoy Hotel, Cairo.
November 15th, 1923.

The Director-General Antiquities Department, Cairo.

TUT·ANKH·AMEN'S TOMB

DEAR SIR,—I have the honour to acknowledge receipt of your letter No. C2 of the 13th inst., and, after careful consideration of the terms, I am prepared to agree to the measures which you propose; but I wish it to be a term of my assent that the present arrangement is without prejudice to such rights as have been ceded to Almina Countess of Carnarvon under the concession, and also that if the Government wish at any time to reconsider the measures now proposed, I should be consulted regarding any changes which the Government may contemplate.

I have the honour to be, dear Sir,
Your obedient Servant,
Signed: HOWARD CARTER.

Wishing to make quite sure that there was no misunderstanding, Mr. Carter left his work again and returned to Cairo on the night of November 14th. On the afternoon of the 15th, accompanied by Mr. Mace, Mr. Carter saw Mr. Tottenham at his house, and handed over to him the letter quoted above, which Mr. Tottenham assured him would be accepted.

On November 17th, thinking that everything was settled, Mr. Carter returned to Luxor and began operations on the tomb.

On November 21st he received a letter from M. Lacau, a letter which shows clearly the thoroughly unpractical and one-sided view insisted upon by the Director-General of the Antiquities Service.

Ministry of Public Works, Cairo

H . CARTER ESQ. November 20th, 1923.

SIR, —I have the honour to acknowledge receipt of
your letter of the 15th instant, in reply to mine of the 13th
instant, and note your assent to the measures proposed by
this Department. As for your reservations of the rights
under the concession of the Countess of Carnarvon, having regard to the fact that the measures foreshadowed are
of a purely administrative character, necessarily falling
within the exclusive jurisdiction of the Egyptian
Government, and do not affect the object of the concession, which is of an essentially scientific nature, granted
for purposes of scientific research, the Government fails to
see its relevance to the measures in question. For the same 22
reason the Egyptian Government, whilst ready and willing
—not only out of courtesy but with a view to facilitating
the execution of the regulations so far as this devolves
upon the concessionnaire—to advise you beforehand of
the measures which it proposes to adopt, cannot admit
any limitation on its own exclusive right to regulate matters of a purely administrative character, such as the carrying into effect of a concession over the Public Domain,
or matters of public policy and of general interest, such as
the access of the public to a part of the State's Domain,
and reports to the public of operations conducted under
the control of the Antiquities Service.

I have already on several occasions expressed to you the same views, but I feel bound to take this opportunity of reiterating and confirming them.

In conclusion, I note that you consider the measures adopted to be workable. As for the reservations you desired to attach to your assent, I feel confident that the reasons to which I have given expression above will convince you that these reservations have no *raison d'être*. I feel equally confident that, quite apart from considerations of a purely legal nature, you will agree with me that the best interests of Lady Carnarvon lie in not shackling in any way the liberty of action of the Government in regulating a totally abnormal situation, which precedent and custom in matters of scientific research could not lead it to foresee—a situation, moreover, to the existence of which the Government has in no way contributed.

I have the honour to be, Sir,
Your obedient Servant,
Signed: P. LACAU,
Director-General Antiquities Department.

Following this, on November 22nd, Mr. Carter received the subjoined two documents, one being a letter from the Under-Secretary of State of the Department of Public Works to M. Lacau, the other a communiqué issued to the public.

C.2/1. November 21st, 1923.

TUT·ANKH·AMEN'S TOMB
MR. CARTER'S COMMUNIQUÉ—PROPOSED METHOD OF TRANSMISSION

Director-General Antiquities Service.

SIR,—With reference to the decision that the Press Bureau will issue regularly in Cairo, early in the morning,

reports about the operations of the previous day, after discussion with Mr. Carter as to the best *modus operandi* to
prevent leakage and to protect the staff of your
Department from unjust charges, I am of opinion that the
best plan will be for Mr. Carter to hand to the Chief
Inspector at Luxor an expanded copy of his telegram to
The Times, not later than 7.30 of the morning following
the dispatch of *The Times* telegram, and for the Chief
Inspector to telegraph it to the Press Bureau in Cairo. The
expanded message will be handed to the Chief Inspector
ready typed on telegram forms for his signature and dispatch. Mr. Carter is prepared to pay the cost of such 23
telegrams, in order to obtain the desired protection from
leakage. This arrangement has the additional advantage
that the communiqués will reach the Press Bureau at an
earlier hour than if sent by post, and obviates the possibility of the communiqué not being posted in time to catch
the 6 P.M. train to Cairo.

Kindly issue instructions for this system to be given a trial. If successful it should be adopted as a permanent arrangement.

I have the honour to be, Sir,
Your obedient Servant,
Signed: P. M. TOTTENHAM,
Under-Secretary of State, P.W.M.

TUT·ANKH·AMEN'S TOMB, 1923-4
COMMUNIQUÉ

The season's work at the Tomb of Tut·ankh·amen has begun, and, as last year, the Press will be supplied, through the Press Bureau in Cairo, with daily news about the progress of the operations. Further facilities to the Press will be given by allowing representative journalists, not exceeding fifteen in number, to visit the Tomb once a fortnight.

The staff of the Antiquities Department in the Valley of the Kings had been strengthened in order to ensure a continuous and close supervision. The Chief Inspector and three Egyptian officials of the Department have been delegated for this purpose.

The unexampled interest shown last year by the public in this Tomb, in Egypt as in other countries, shows signs of continuing into this season, and the Ministry of Public Works would have liked to accord facilities for visiting it to a considerable number of visitors. But, unless the work of emptying the Tomb is to suffer almost interminable delay, and the safety of these most valuable finds is to be gravely endangered, permits to visitors must—and will—be ruthlessly limited. It is hoped the public will see that this strict limitation of facilities for visitors is by no means arbitrary, but is conditioned by the very nature of the work. The Tomb consists of four chambers—viz. the antechamber, which was cleared last year; a small room leading off it—the door of which is bricked up; the large chamber now filled by the nested canopies; and a fourth room which cannot be opened till next season, 1924-25.

The winter's work will consist in the removal of the canopies, till the coffin—which, as is supposed, lies untouched in their centre—is reached. Plank by plank these great boxes must be taken to pieces, without losing any of the decoration they may be found to bear. There must be room to manipulate them and get them out. The manoeuvre, however, is more difficult today than when the ancient Egyptians got them in. Damage is now irreparable, and the objects are not as stout and solid as they once were. In these three thousand years the wood

> has shrunk; the decorated plaster has not, and in places will have buckled and detached itself from its support. The pressure of a finger would fracture it.
>
> With barely room, then, to manipulate the beams, 24
> with an inadequate supply of air, with the heat of the powerful electric lights, the work will be found extremely trying. If it is carried on into the summer, difficulties will be vastly increased, as anyone who has been in the Valley of the Kings can testify.
>
> Now, each party of visitors who interrupts the work for a day (and it is not possible to admit such parties without interrupting the work) compels the diggers to work one more day into the heat.
>
> Appeal is therefore confidently made to all men of good will not to ask for a favour which costs so much to grant.
>
> However, and in order to satisfy the legitimate curiosity of the public both Egyptian and foreign, arrangements will be made so that, when the removal of the great shrines has so far progressed that it becomes materially practicable for strangers to enter, and there is something of real interest for them to see, work will be interrupted for a week or more—probably in January—and visitors, in numbers fixed by the Ministry of Public Works, will be admitted on presentation of special tickets. Notice of the dates fixed for these visits will be issued in ample time.

With regard to the first of these documents the point should be emphasized that, wishing to assure the satisfactory carrying out of the programme, Mr. Carter burdened his expedition with the various extra expenses thus entailed.

The second document was eminently reasonable and fair, but it was negatived as time proceeded by the fact that a large number of permits and requests, other than those of the Press, were issued by the Government. At the same time there were certain visitors for diplomatic and political reasons Mr. Carter could not well refuse; and, moreover, whenever it was possible without causing serious delay to the work, he extended all courtesy to Egyptian notables and their families, considering that they, of all people, had most right to visit the Tomb. It may be added in this connexion that Mr. Carter was on one occasion severely criticised by an official of the Department for having permitted the Mudir (Governor) of the Province to enter the Tomb.

On November 27th a new surprise was sprung upon Mr. Carter while in Luxor on the weekly rest-day. In the course of a conversation with Mr. Engelbach, Chief Inspector of Antiquities for the district, he was informed that it was the intention of the Government to ask him for a complete list of his collaborators. This new demand became official on December 2nd when he received the following letter from Mr. Quibell:—

DEAR CARTER, Helouan, 1.12.23.

The Minister wants a list of your staff—why, I don't know. I could have written it out almost, but not quite, for you may have people coming out of whom I don't know the names, and I'm not sure of Callendar's name, nor of Mr. Bethell's initials, and so on.

25 So would you correct and complete this list and send it to me? and I will transmit it. I'm late with it. We have been busy and I'm sadly in arrears. Lythgoe turned up to-day.

Yours as ever,

Signed: J. E. QUIBELL.

H. Carter.
A. C. Mace.
H. Burton.
A. Lucas.

—Callendar.
Dr. Alex. Scott.
The Hon. — Bethell.
Sir Archibald Reid.
Prof. Derry.

P.S.—Among the things newly put out, an ivory box particularly charmed me. I had not heard of it before. —

J. E. Q.

This demand was so extraordinary, and so entirely unprecedented in the whole history of Egyptian excavation, that Mr. Carter was at a loss to know what the purpose of it might be. He accordingly wrote the following two letters, one to the Minister, the other to Mr. Quibell:—

Luxor,
December 3rd, 1923.

H.E. Abdel Hamid Suleman Pasha,
Minister of Public Works Department, Cairo.

YOUR EXCELLENCY,

I have the honour to enclose a copy of a letter I have just received from Mr. Quibell, of the Antiquities Department.

I am rather puzzled as to what the request can mean, for surely in the details of my work I am at liberty to employ whomever I wish, so long as I adhere to the terms of my concession.

Believe me,
Your Excellency,
Yours sincerely,
Signed: HOWARD CARTER.

Luxor,
December 4th, 1923.

DEAR QUIBELL,

I am in receipt of your letter of December 1st, asking for a list of my staff.

It seems an extraordinary request.

As you state you did not know the purpose of this request, I have written, to save time, to H.E. the Minister, who, according to your letter, requires the information.

Yours sincerely,
Signed: HOWARD CARTER.

26 In reply he received the following letter from M. Lacau on December 11th:

Direction Générale du Service des Antiquités,
NO. 27-2/5. Le Caire,
10 Décembre, 1923.

MONSIEUR,

S.E. le Ministre des Travaux Publics me charge de vous informer officiellement de la décision qu'il a prise en ce qui concerne la question de vos collaborateurs.

Son Excellence veut avoir la liste de *tous vos collaborateurs* et se réserve d'approuver ou de refuser la présence de telle ou telle personne parmi ces collaborateurs. Ce droit d'acceptation des collaborateurs découle logiquement du droit de contrôle matériel et scientifique sur toute fouille que l'on ne saurait contester au Gouvernement.

Voudrez vous croire, Monsieur, etc.,
Le Directeur Général.
Signé: P. LACAU.

Monsieur H. Carter,
Représentant de Lady Carnarvon, à Luxor.

[General Direction of the Antiquities Service
NO. 27-2/5 *Cairo, 10 December, 1923.*
SIR,

H. E. the Minister for Public Works has asked me to inform you officially of the decision which he has taken on the matter of your collaborators.

His Excellency would like to have a list of all your collaborators, *and reserves the right to approve or to refuse the presence of any one of the collaborators. This right of acceptance of collaborators stems logically from the Government's unquestionable right of material and scientific control over the whole excavation.*

Please believe, Sir, etc.,
The Director General.
Signed: P. LACAU

Mr H. Carter,
Representative of Lady Carnarvon, at Luxor.]

Subsequent events showed clearly enough the real purpose of this demand. The opposition Press had evidently been complaining to the Minister again on the subject of Mr. Merton, and the Minister and M. Lacau thought they saw an opportunity of getting rid of him in this way.

On the same day Mr. Carter also received the subjoined lengthy communication from M. Lacau, enclosing an entirely new form of authorization for his concession, drawn up by the Department to cover the arbitrary measures it proposed to take:—

Direction Générale du Service des Antiquités,
NO. 18-14/1 Le Caire, le 10 Decembre, 1923.
MONSIEUR,

S.E. le Ministre des Travaux Publics me charge de vous informer officiellement de la décision qu'il a prise en ce qui concerne la question des visiteurs dans *la tombe Tout·ankh·Amon.*

Personne ne peut visiter la tombe sans une autorisation écrite du Gouvernement. Cette mesure est indispensable pour assurer la bonne marche du travail. Après examen approfondi de la question, le Gouvernement estime que le droit d'accès au chantier appartient logiquement aux seule travailleurs qualifiés accompagnant le fouilleur. Une fouille ne pouvant avoir d'autre but que la recherche scientifique et non la satisfaction d'une vaine curiosité, nous devons assurer et, au besoin, imposer au fouiller des conditions de travail qui sauvegardent pleinement les résultats scientifiques.

27 Dans la pratique, pour éviter un échange de lettres et de dépêches avec le Caire, notre representant à Louxor, Mr. R. Engelbach, aura en main 15 ou 20 autorisations en blanc, signée par nous, dont il pourra user pour faire entrer certaines personnalités (entre autres les archéologues, les haut fonctionnaires et les amis de Lord Carnarvon), auxquels nous accorderions sans hésiter l'accès de la tombe. Il sera juge: renvoyez lui donc les demandes que l'on vous adresse. Bien entendu, chaque fois qu'il y a hésitation possible, il en référera au Service.

Cette mesure, comme toutes les autres que nous n'avions pas eu l'occasion de prendre par le passé, est imposée au Gouvernement par l'état de choses créé par le mouvement extraordinaire de curiosité qui a été suscité autour des fouilles du tombeau de Tut·ank·Amon. Le Gouvernement estime que, malgré ce mouvement, les fouilles doivent s'exécuter dans les conditions normales de tranquillité et de sérieux qui sont exigées par leur caractère scientifique et qui sont particulièrement désirables lorsqu'il s'agit d'une pareille découverte.

Au surplus, instruit par l'expérience des derniers évènements, le Gouvernement a tenu, en vue d'éviter de vaines et pénibles discussions et de prévenir à tout jamais la création d'un semblable état de choses, à réviser sa formule d'autorisation de fouilles, en précisant d'une façon explicite les droits de l'Etat sur tous les chantiers de fouilles.

Vous trouverez ci-joint un exemplaire de cette nouvelle formule d'autorisation qui sera employée à l'avenir.

Comme vous le voyez, il n'y a rien, dans tout ce que nous avons été obligés de faire, qui vous touche personnellement. Les fouilles de Tout·ankh·amon, avec tout de bruit qui a été fait autour d'elles, ont contraint le Gouvernement à prendre des mesures qu'il n'avait jamais eu l'occasion de prendre jusqu'ici.

Je vous serais reconnaissant de vouloir bien donner suite sans délai à la décision de S.E. le Ministre. Ces discussions nous ont pris ainsi qu'à vous-mêmes beaucoup plus de temps qu'il n'était nécessaire, et le Gouvernement ne discute plus, mais vous transmet sa décision.

Voudrez croire, Monsieur, l'assurance de mes sentiments très distingués.

Le Directeur Général,
Signé: P. LACAU

Monsieur H. Carter,
Représentant de Lady Carnarvon,
Louxor.

[*General Direction of the Antiquities Service,*
NO. 18-14/1 *Cairo, 10 December, 1923.*
SIR,

H.E. the Minister of Public Works has asked me to inform you formally of the decision which he has taken in relation to visitors to the tomb of Tout·ankh·Amon.

No one may visit the tomb without the written authorization of the Government. This measure is essential to ensure the smooth operation of the work. Having looked thoroughly into the matter, the Government believes that only qualified workers accompanying the excavator should have access to the work. As the aim of an excavation should be only scientific research and not the satisfaction of vain curiosity, we must ensure and, if necessary, impose on the excavator, working conditions which entirely safeguard the scientific results.

In practice, in order to avoid an exchange of letters and telegrams with Cairo, our representative in Luxor, Mr. R. Engelbach, will have in hand 15 or 20 blank authorizations, signed by us, which he may use to allow access to the tomb to certain persons (among others archaeologists, high civil servants and friends of Lord Carnarvon). He will be the judge: send him any requests that are made to you. Of course, if in doubt, he will refer the matter to the Ministry.

This measure, as all the others which we have not had occasion to take in the past, is imposed on the Government by the situation created by the extraordinary curiosity which has arisen around the tomb of Tout·ankh·Amon. The Government believes that, despite this curiosity, the clearance must be carried out in normal, peaceful and serious conditions, which are justified by its scientific nature and are required in the context of such a discovery.

Furthermore, learning from the experience of past events, the Government is set, in order to avoid the pointless and laborious discussions and to prevent a similar situation ever occurring again, to revise its form of authorization to excavate, setting out explicitly the rights of the State over all excavation sites.

You will find herewith an example of this new form of authorization which will be used in the future.

As you will see, nothing in the measures which we have had to take affects you personally. The Tout·ankh·-Amon excavations, with all the fuss which has been made around them, have forced the Government to take measures which it has never had to take before.

I should be grateful if you would implement without delay the decision of H.E. the Minister. These discussions have taken us, as yourself, much more time than required, and the Government refuses to discuss the issue any further but hereby conveys its decision.

Please be assured, Sir, of my distinguished consideration.

The Director General,

Signed: P. LACAU

Mr H. Carter,
Representative of Lady Carnarvon,
Luxor.]

MINISTÈRE DES TRAVAUX PUBLICS
DIRECTION GÉNÉRALE DES ANTIQUITÉS.

LE MINISTRE DES TRAVAUX PUBLICS,

Sur la proposition de M. le Directeur Général du Service des Antiquités, et conformément à l'avis favorable du Comité d'Egyptologie, accorde aux termes et conditions ci-dessous édictés la présente.

AUTORISATION DE FOUILLES 28

M. ....

agissant en qualité de représentant de ....

....

..................................(Institution ou Mission scientifique) ci-après appelée le bénéficiaire de l'autorisation, et ce suivant pouvoir dont expédition en bonne et due forme a été par lui remise au Service des Antiquités, est autorisé à exécuter des fouilles scientifiques à ....

....

.... (Localité, Markaz, Moudirieh)

....

sur tous les terrains appartenant à l'Etat, situés dans les limites ci-dessous désignées:

....

....

et indiquées au plan ci-annexé.

La présente autorisation est délivrée en conformité de la Loi No. 14 de 1912 sur les Antiquités, ainsi que le 1. Arrêté Ministeriel No. 52 en date du Décembre, 1912, portant Règlement sur les Fouilles.

L'autorisation, qui est personnelle, ne pourra, en aucun cas et sous aucune forme, être cédée en tout ou en partie à des tiers.

Elle est, en outre, délivrée aux risques et périls exclusifs du bénéficiaire de l'autorisation et sous la réserve expresse et absolue des droits des tiers et sans responsabilités aucune pour le Gouvernement Egyptien.

Art. 2. La présente autorisation est donnée pour une période de .... (saison ou partie de saison) commençant le .... et venant à expiration le ....

Elle ne pourra être renouvelée que conformément aux dispositions de l'Art. 16 de l'Arrêté Ministériel susvisé.

Art. 3. Les fouilles seront exécutées sous la direction de M. .... représentant le bénéficiaire de l'autorisation.

Tout changement éventuel dans la personne chargée

de la direction des fouilles devra être accepté par écrit par le Directeur Générale du Service des Antiquités.

De même tout le personnel de direction, d'études et d'exécution attaché aux fouilles devra être nominativement et par écrit approuvé par le Service des Antiquités, qui pourra à tout moment ordonner l'éloignement du chantier de fouilles de toute personne dont la présence lui paraîtrait indésirable.

Art. 4. Le chantier des fouilles est en principe réservé au personnel du bénéficiaire de l'autorisation ainsi qu'aux agents du Service des Antiquités. Le Service des Antiquités se réserve d'interdire l'accès du chantier à tous les visiteurs quels qu'ils soient. Il se réserve de même le droit exclusif de délivrer des autorisations de visite aux personnes étrangères aux fouilles et au Service.

Art. 5. Le Service des Antiquités exercera sur le 29
chantier par l'entremise de ses agents son droit de surveillance tant au point de vue de la sécurité matérielle et de la conservation des lieux et des objets trouvés, qu'au point de vue de la conduite scientifiques des fouilles. Le bénéficiaire de l'autorisation ainsi que son représentant ou tout autre de ses agents devront exécuter les instructions qu'ils recevront et ne devront apporter aucune entrave à l'exécution des mesures que le Service des Antiquités croira devoir prendre à cet effet.

Art. 6. Aucune construction ne pourra être élevée sur le terrain auquel s'applique la présente autorisation sans une permission spéciale et écrite du Directeur Général du Service des Antiquités at aux conditions qui y seront déterminées.

Toute construction qui serait élevée en contravention de la présente disposition devra être immédiatement démolie sous peine, en cas de refus, du retrait de la présente autorisation à prononcer dans les formes réglementaires.

Art. 7. Le droit de publication des résultats scientifiques est réservé au bénéficiaire de l'autorisation, mais le Gouvernement pourra toujours, s'il le juge utile, publier lui-même tous les faits d'intérêt général et non scientifique concernant la fouille. Il est seul juge d'ailleurs, en ce point, du caractère des communications qu'il croira devoir faire au public.

Art. 8. Toutes les antiquités trouvées pendant toute la durée des travaux seront remises au Service des Antiquités pour être partagées entre ce dernier et le bénéficiaire de l'autorisation, conformément à la Loi sur les Antiquités et aux dispositions du Règlement sur les Fouilles.

Art. 9. Le droit de reproduction commerciale des objets trouvés au cours de fouilles et revenant au Service des Antiquités est réservé au Gouvernement Egyptien.

Art. 10. Le bénéficiaire de l'autorisation s'engage à publier d'une manière scientifique le resultat de ses fouilles dans un délai raisonnable. Tout retard exagéré peut entraîner le refus de toute nouvelle autorisation.

Art. 11. En cas de contravention à l'une quelconque des conditions de la présente autorisation, les travaux pourront être suspendus par la Direction Générale du Service des Antiquités ou par tout agent du Service autorisé à cet effet, jusqu'à ce que l'état de contravention ait cessé. L'autorisation pourra même être retirée, en cas de contravention grave, par Arrêté de S.E. le Ministre des Travaux Publics, pris sur avis motive du Comité d'Egyptologie appuyé par le Directeur Général (Art. 17 du Règlement sur les Fouilles).

Delivré au le Caire, le ....

Pour proposition

LE MINISTRE DES TRAVAUX PUBLICS.

LE DIRECTEUR GÉNÉRAL DES ANTIQUITÉS.
LE BÉNÉFICIAIRE DE L'AUTORISATION.

[MINISTRY OF PUBLIC WORKS
ANTIQUITIES SERVICE
THE MINISTER OF PUBLIC WORKS,
At the suggestion of the Director General of Antiquities, and by virtue of the favourable advice of the Committee of Egyptology, grants under the terms and conditions set out below the following:

AUTHORIZATION TO EXCAVATE

M. ....
acting as the representative of ....
....
.... *(institution or scientific mission)* *hereafter referred to as the holder of the authorization, and by virtue of the authority which in good and due form has been given to him by the Antiquities Service, is authorized to carry out scientific excavations at* ....
....
.... *(location, Markaz, Moudirieh)*
....
on all the land belonging to the State, within the limits designated below:
....
and indicated on the attached plan.

The present Authorization is delivered under Law no. 14 of 1912 on Antiquities, and under 1. Ministerial decree no. 52 dated December 1912, relating to the Regulations applying to Excavations.

The Authorization, which is personal, may not, in any case or in any form, be transferred in whole or in part to a third party.

It is, furthermore, delivered at the exclusive risk and

peril of the holder of the authorization without prejudice to the rights of third parties and without any responsibility for the Egyptian Government.

Art. 2. The present authorization is granted for a period of .... (season or part of a season) commencing the .... and expiring the ....

It may only be renewed in accordance with the arrangements of Art. 16 of the Ministerial decree referred to above.

Art. 3. The excavations will take place under the direction of Mr .... representing the holder of the authorization.

Any change of the person in charge of the direction of the excavations shall be subject to the prior written approval of the Director General of Antiquities.

Similarly, all persons involved in the direction, study, and execution of the excavations must be named and shall be subject to the prior written approval of the Antiquities Service, which may at any time order the removal from the site of any person whose presence seems to the Service to be undesirable.

Art. 4. Right of access to the excavation site is in principle reserved to the personnel of the holder of the authorization as well as the agents of the Antiquities Service. The Antiquities Service reserves the right to forbid access to the site to all visitors whoever they may be. Furthermore, the Antiquities Service reserves the exclusive right to allocate visitors' permits to strangers to the excavation and to the Service.

Art 5. The Antiquities Service through its agents will exercise on the site its right to supervise the security of the site and conservation of the objects found therein as well as the conduct of the excavations. The holder of the authorization, likewise his representative and all his agents, must carry out the instructions which they receive and must not hinder in any way the execution of the measures which the Antiquities Service believes should be taken to this effect.

Art 6. Any construction raised on the site which is the subject of this authorization shall be subject to the Director General of Antiquities' prior written consent.

Any construction which is raised in breach of this provision must be immediately demolished under penalty, in case of refusal, of the withdrawal of the present authorization, which shall take place within legal time limits.

Art 7. The publication rights to the scientific results is reserved to the holder of the authorization, but the Government may, if deemed necessary, publish all the facts of general and non-scientific interest concerning the excavation. In this respect the Government shall be the judge of the type of communications which it believes it should publish.

Art. 8. Any antiquities found during the entire duration of the works shall be given to the Antiquities Service to be divided between the latter and the holder of the authorization, in accordance with the Antiquities Law and its provisions on the Regulation relating to Excavations.

Art. 9. The right of commercial reproduction of objects found in the course of excavation, which objects are due to the Antiquities Service, shall belong to the Egyptian Government.

Art. 10. The holder of the authorization undertakes to publish in scientific form the results of his excavations after a reasonable interval. Any extreme delay could result in the refusal of any new authorization.

Art. 11. In the case of the breach of any one of the conditions of the present authorization, the works may be suspended by the Director General of the Antiquities Service or by any agent of the Service authorized to that effect, until the state of contravention has ceased. The authorization can also be withdrawn, in the case of a serious breach, by decree of H.E. the Minister of Public Works, taken on the advice of the Committee of Egyptology supported by the Director General (Art. 17 of the Regulation relating to Excavations).

Delivered in Cairo, the ....

For proposal.

THE MINISTER OF PUBLIC WORKS
THE DIRECTOR GENERAL OF ANTIQUITIES
THE HOLDER OF THE AUTHORIZATION]

It had been gradually becoming apparent that the Government were desirous of assuming complete control of the work, and in
30 these two documents their real attitude is quite clear. '*Le Gouvernement ne discute plus, mais vous transmet sa décision*' ['The Government refuses to discuss the issue any further, but conveys to you its decision'].

This *décision*, as a study of the new authorization will show, involves the following points;—

1. The concessionnaire is to submit to the Government a full list of his collaborators, the Government reserving themselves the right to strike out any name they please.

2. The concessionnaire must not admit anyone to the tomb, not even a visiting archaeologist, whether for expert advice or otherwise, without first submitting the name to the Government, and obtaining their permission.

The futility of this becomes evident when one remembers that the archaeologist in question may only be in Luxor for twenty-four hours. Moreover the new clause involves a distinct breach of the concessionnaire's rights with regard to the proper method of scientific work.

3. The concessionnaire, while obliged to shoulder the complete responsibility of the undertaking, and to defray its entire cost, is to have no real control of the work itself, but is to be at the absolute mercy of the Government official placed in charge.

4. The Government reserves to itself the right of making public the results of his excavations.

It is unanimously agreed amongst archaeologists that restrictions such as these, if carried into effect, would wreck the whole future of archaeology in the country, and, in the interest of science alone, Mr. Carter could not subscribe to anything that would establish such an unfortunate precedent.

In the present case, moreover, such new restrictions cannot apply, for, by Mr. Lacau's own admission in the authorization of July 12th, 1923, Almina Countess of Carnarvon is given the right to finish the work under the terms of the original concession.

For these obvious reasons Mr. Carter felt that not only could he not agree to such unreasonable demands, but that he must make a definite protest against them.

On December 12th M. Lacau came to Luxor, and an incident occurred which, though trivial in itself, throws a significant light on the reason for the Government's attitude, in this particular case, with regard to the question of collaborators.

Mr. Carter was indisposed on that day, and obliged to remain in his house. The tomb being thus closed, M. Lacau made a visit to the Laboratory and there met Mr. Merton, and remarked to him that he was the cause of the past trouble, and that more was to follow.

On December 13th M. Lacau made Mr. Carter an official visit at 9 A.M. with reference to the two documents quoted above. Mr. Carter pointed out that these new demands on the part of the Government were unjustifiable, and an encroachment on his rights under the original concession, and that for that reason there was no other course open to him but to refuse to accede to them.

M. Lacau subsequently paid a visit to the tomb with Mr. Carter, and then left for Cairo.

On December 15th Mr. Carter received a telegraphic communication from Mr. Tottenham, asking him to go to Cairo to see the Minister.

31 On the night of December 17th, accompanied by Mr. Merton, Mr. Carter left for Cairo.

It may be stated here that on this day the regular Press visit took place, and that there visited the tomb eight persons, only one of whom represented an Egyptian paper, and he not a *bona fide* correspondent.

In friendly conversations which he had with both Mr. Tottenham at his house and with the Minister of the Department of Public Works at the Ministry, it became clear to Mr. Carter that the demand with regard to the collaborators was directed solely against Mr. Merton. The Minister urged that the questions of visitors and of Mr. Merton were the cause of undue criticism on the part of the Press, and that he had the intention, upon receiving a list of Mr. Carter's staff, to strike off Mr. Merton, whom he said he could not disassociate from *The Times*. When Mr. Carter explained his exact position in the matter—that Mr. Merton was a member of the staff, seconded to him by *The Times*, and that the whole of the Press news went in his own name, he (Mr. Merton) not being allowed to send any telegram other than those signed by Mr. Carter—the Minister asked Mr. Carter nevertheless to prevent Mr. Merton from entering the tomb except on Press days.

Mr. Carter pointed out that by accepting this and other Government proposals he would be establishing a wrong precedent. Before giving a final decision, however, he suggested that he be given time to confer with his collaborators.

The following morning (December 19th) Mr. Carter went to

the Ministry again, and informed His Excellency that he regretted that, after very careful consideration, he could not conform with his wish on these points, and must hold to the terms of his original concession. At the Minister's request this reply was put into writing, and submitted to him through the proper channels.

Continental-Savoy Hotel, Cairo.
Dec. 20, 1923.

THE DIRECTOR-GENERAL,
ANTIQUITIES SERVICE, CAIRO.
DEAR SIR,

Your letter of December 10th, No. 27.2/5 and 18.14/1.

In confirmation of my interview with you at Luxor on the 13th inst., and of my subsequent interviews with H.E. the Minister of Public Works here in Cairo on the 18th and 19th inst., I regret that I cannot see my way to conform to the restrictions you seek to impose upon me.

You will remember that early in the season the whole question was thoroughly thrashed out. We then came to an amicable arrangement which I have faithfully carried out, and I fail to see why these further questions should be raised.

The carrying out of the proposals made to me would, in fact, prejudice and be an infringement of the rights of the *concessionnaires*, and I must insist on being allowed to conduct the work in the Tomb in accordance with the legal rights with which I am invested under the terms of the original concession.

Further, I must point out that the proposals contained in the correspondence received this month from your Service, to publish Tut·ankh·amen material in the Cairo Museum Guide Book, is a direct infringement of our
rights under the concession, and I must warn you that if, 32

as you threaten, you ignore my protest I shall reluctantly be compelled to take action in defence of the interests of the executors of the late Lord Carnarvon.

I am, dear Sir,
Yours faithfully.
Signed: HOWARD CARTER.

This letter was posted between the hours of 2 and 3 in the afternoon of December 20th, and at 4.5 P.M. Mr. Carter was summoned to the telephone at his hotel, and had a conversation with Mr. Tottenham, of which the following is a summary:—

Continental Hotel, Cairo.
20-12-23 4.5 P.M.

[*Memorandum*]

MEMORIZED SUMMARY OF TELEPHONE MESSAGE FROM TOTTENHAM TO HOWARD CARTER

T. I have been talking to H.E, and ask you not to send the letter you propose sending, as H.E. has been in consultation with the Committee of Contentieux, and their decision is to close the Tomb. I pointed out to H.E. what disastrous results this would mean, and as he (H.E.) is only asking a very small point from you—i.e. in regard to Merton not entering the Tomb—he thinks you could reconsider it.

H. C. My letter is already written and posted.

T. Very well; I can return that letter to you and say nothing more about it.

H. C. Unfortunately all my telegrams have been sent to England and various machinery set in motion.

T. Are you quite sure you have sent the letter?

H. C. Yes.

The same question asked again, and the same answer.

T. again pointed out the small point that H.E. required, reminding me at the same time that the Government was within its rights regarding a list of my staff for purely Government control purposes, and adding that I might have possibly a thief amongst my staff. He thought this would put me in a very wrong position and cause the matter to assume grave proportions.

H. C. I have fully considered all the aspects of the case, and in loyalty to my scientific colleagues and to science in general I am unable to act otherwise.

T. You are going up to Luxor to-night, are you not?

H. C. Yes.

This ended the conversation.

It should be remembered that in this conversation Mr. Tottenham makes the statement that the Government were only asking one small concession, that with regard to Mr. Merton, though as a matter of fact this was only one of the many issues raised in the foregoing documents.

In the intervals of these Government negotiations Mr. Carter
had been proceeding with the heavy work of dismantling the
shrines, and by January 3rd he had arrived at a point where he
might be able to open the remaining shrine doors. If this should 33
prove possible, he would find out whether there was a sarcophagus within, and get some idea of the problem that lay before him.
He therefore wrote the following note to Mr. Engelbach:—

Luxor,
Jan. 3, 1924.

DEAR ENGELBACH,

I should be pleased if you could come over this afternoon about 3.45.

I find that I shall be able to make an interesting

experiment which I think would interest you to see.

Yours sincerely,

Signed: HOWARD CARTER.

Previous to that, in a conversation Mr. Carter had had with Mr. Engelbach in the tomb itself, the latter expressed a wish to be present when the doors of the shrines were opened, and, to obviate the question of leakage of news, had said that he would come by himself without an Egyptian inspector. Mr. Carter had replied to him that that was a matter for him to consider, but that it would give Mr. Carter great pleasure if he would be present at such an interesting investigation.

This conversation actually occurred while Mr. Carter was wrapping up the pall structure to protect it during removal.

On January 3rd at 3 P.M. this experiment was carried out. Mr. Engelbach was present together with a group of the leading archaeologists then in Luxor, who, as on similar occasions in the past, had been invited by Mr. Carter to witness the proceedings.

Following on this ceremony the subjoined three telegrams passed:—

[*Telegrams*]—

LACAU, Museum, Cairo.

Investigations to-day enabled me to ascertain that the four shrines contain a magnificent sarcophagus intact regards.

CARTER. Jan. 3, 1924.

CARTER, Luxor.

Très heureux cordiales félicitations prière prévenir par lettre date probable ouverture couvercle ne pourrai allé avant.

LACAU. Jan. 5, 1924.

[*CARTER, Luxor.*

Very happy many congratulations please inform me by letter probable date of opening lid will not be able to come before then.

LACAU. Jan. 5, 1924]

LACAU, Museum, Cairo.

Merci votre très amiable dépêche vous préviendrai d'avance date ouverture aussitôt fixée.

CARTER. Jan. 5, 1924.

[*LACAU, Museum, Cairo.*

Thank you for your very kind telegram will inform you in advance date of opening as soon as fixed.

CARTER. Jan. 5, 1924.]

On January 5th Mr. Tottenham made a special visit to the tomb, and informed Mr. Carter that the Minister had received a telegram from Mr. Bradstreet, of the *Morning Post,* stating that Mr. Carter had allowed Mr. Moyne, a representative of *The Times*, to enter the tomb, and that in consequence the Egyptian Government was about to take drastic measures.

Mr. Tottenham also stated that a further complication had
arisen from the fact that Mr. Carter had opened the doors of the
shrines and exposed the sarcophagus (P.M. Jan. 3rd) without an
Egyptian inspector being present. This was hardly Mr. Carter's 34
business, as the Chief Inspector had been informed and was present himself.

With regard to the accusation that he had taken Mr. Moyne into the tomb, Mr. Carter asked Mr. Tottenham whether it would not have been fairer to have taken steps to find out whether the accusation was true. In point of fact it was absolutely untrue, for Mr. Moyne had not entered the tomb, nor had Mr. Carter ever invited him.

As a result of this conversation it is believed that Mr. Tottenham sent a telegram to the Minister asking him to cancel the drastic action he proposed. There was no further move on the part of the Government until January 11th, when Mr. Carter received the following letter:—

MINISTRY OF PUBLIC WORKS
SERVICE DES ANTIQUITÉS .

State Legal Department, Public Works and War.

No. 27.2/5 Le Caire, le 10 Janvier, 1924.

MONSIEUR,

Par votre du 20 Décembre dernier vous refusez d'admettre les demandes formulées dans nos trois lettres—

10 du Décembre, 1923, No. 18.14/4, concernant le contrôle des visites.

20 du Décembre, 1923, No. 27.2/5, la liste de vos collaborateurs.

30 du Décembre, 1923, No. 30.53/32, concernant la publication des notice sur les objets de la tombe dans le Guide de Musée.

Personnellement, je regrette vivement ce refus. C'est la première fois que le Gouvernement Egyptien a des difficultés à propos des fouilles. Ces difficultés ne laissent cependant pas de surprendre. Car quelque laconique qu'il fut, le renouvellement d'autorisation accordé à Lady Carnarvon assurait au Gouvernement la haute surveillance sur les travaux des fouilles. Ce droit découlait, du reste, pour lui, de son droit général de police ainsi que de son droit sur les objets trouvés qui font partie du Domaine Public. Si donc le Service des Antiquités n'a pas eu, lors de ce renouvellement, le souci de régler en détail les différentes questions qui, déjà, dès l'année dernière ne cessaient de provoquer des discussions continues, ce fut uniquement dans la conviction que, grâce à la bonne volonté avec laquelle de part et d'autre on abordait ce renouvellement, aucune difficulté n'était à prévoir. L'attente fut malheureusement déçue. Il semble même que vous donniez à l'autorisation une interprétation qui serait de nature à mettre en échec les mesures que le Gouvernement estime nécessaire de prendre.

Devant cette attitude, j'ai cru devoir recourir à S.E. le Ministre pour qu'il décide les conditions qui doivent être observées dans l'usage de votre autorisation au sujet des questions en suspens, en le priant de vouloir bien tenir compte du fait qu'il serait opportun, pour vous laisser continuer vos travaux cet hiver, de ne pas exercer nos droits dans toute leur étendue.

Voici ce que S.E. le Ministre a décidé après nouvel examen et avis du Contentieux de l'Etat:

1e. *Pour les visites*—Le Ministère maintient son droit de contrôle, mais ce contrôle s'exercera de la façon suivante:

Outre les autorisations du Ministère qu'il continuera à donner comme il l'a fait jusqu'à présent, vous aurez la faculté d'admettre des visiteurs en nombre très restreint, sans qu'ils soient munis d'un permis du Ministère, à condition que vous nous donnerez chaque semaine la liste nominative des personnes que vous aurez admises dans la tombe, avec indication du but de leur visite. En cas de refus de nous communiquer cette liste ou si le nombre des visites nous paraît abusif, nous interdirons toute visite.

2e. *Pour la liste des collaborateurs*—Son Excellence ayant pris connaissance des noms de tous vos collaborateurs n'entend plus obtenir la liste qui avait été demandée. Toutefois, il se réserve pour l'année prochaine de vous en demander communication avant le commencement des travaux. Une clause spéciale dans ce sens figurera dans la nouvelle formule d'autorisation qui sera signée desormais par tous les fouilleurs.

3e. *Pour la publication des notices dans le Guide*—Ni votre droit de publication ni aucun usage en la matière ne sauraient faire échec soit au droit du Gouvernement Egyptien de mettre sur le objets exposés dans le Musée (qui sont du Domaine Public) des notices pour éclairer le public, soit à son droit de publier ces notices dans le Guide de Musée. Ces notices seront donc publiée dans la nouvelle édition du Guide.

Par ces décisions, Son Excellence a tenu à vous donner une preuve de son esprit de conciliation, mais il entend le cas échéant faire respecter sa décision.

Je regrette que votre refus nous ait obligé d'avoir recours encore une fois à la decision de S.E. le Ministre, mais il est agréable, à cette occasion, d'ajouter qu'au point de vue du travail scientifique je suis d'accord avec vous et je ne puis qu'approuver vos méthodes.

En ce qui concerne la reprise du travail l'année prochaine, elle se fera en vertu d'un nouveau modèle de contrat que vous aurez à signer comme tous vos collègues et qui précisera les droits que le Gouvernement entend se réserver sur les chantiers de fouilles.

Il est, en effet, indispensable, étant donnée l'expérience de ces deux dernières années, que toutes les questions contestées et d'autres encore soient prévues à l'avenir dans les autorisations pour recevoir les solutions concrètes qui sauvegarderont l'intérêt du Gouvernement.

Est-il besoin de dire que j'espère n'avoir jamais à exercer tous les droits que nous nous reservons, mais puisqu'il peut y avoir contestation sur des points qui nous paraîssaient clairs, il importent de les rendre plus clairs encore dans un texte écrit. C'est là le but du nouveau modèle d'autorisation. Le texte que je vous avais communiqué n'est pas encore arrêté, mais l'esprit en est clair. Nous en communiquerons très prochainement la rédaction définitive à tous nos collègues.

Veuillez agréer, Monsieur, l'assurance de mes sentiments très distingués.

Signé: LE DIRECTEUR GENÉRAL.

[MINISTRY OF PUBLIC WORKS
ANTIQUITES SERVICE.

State Legal Department, Public Works and War.

No. 27.2/5 *Cairo, 10th January, 1924.*

SIR.

In yours of 20th December last you refuse to admit the demands laid out in our three letters—

10th December, 1923, No. 18. 14/4, concerning the control of visits.

20th December, 1923, No. 27.2/5, the list of your collaborators.

30th December, 1923, No. 30.53/32, concerning the publication of the objects from the tomb in the Museum Guide.

Personally I very much regret this refusal. This is the first time that the Egyptian Government has had such difficulties concerning excavations. These difficulties are surprising. The renewal of the authorization granted to Lady Carnarvon ensured for the Government the ultimate supervision of the excavation works. This right stems, above all, from the Government's general policing right and also from its right over objects discovered which are as such in the Public Domain. If the Antiquities Service did not have, when it was renewed, the solicitude to settle in detail the various questions which, already from the previous year, had provoked continuing discussions, this was uniquely in the conviction that, thanks to the good-will with which the renewal was approached, no difficulties were foreseen. This expectation was unfortunately not borne out. It also seems that you give the authorization an interpretation which is of a nature to ensure the failure of the measures which the Government judges necessary.

Faced with this attitude, I felt I had to have recourse to H.E. the Minister and to ask him to define the condition in which your authorisation would be granted. I have also asked His Excellency to bear in mind, when defining the conditions, that you should be able to continue your excavation this winter.

Here is what H.E. the Minister has decided after new examination and advice from the Contentieux de l'Etat:

1. Regarding visits—*the Minister maintains his right of control, but this control will be exercised as follows:*

In addition to the authorization of the Ministry which the Minister will continue to grant, you will have the right to admit visitors in very limited numbers, without a permit from the Minister, conditional upon your giving us each week a list of people whom you have admitted to the tomb with an indication of the aims of their visits. If you refuse to give us this list or if the number of visits seems to us excessive, all visits will be forbidden.

2. As to the list of collaborators—*His Excellency, aware of the names of all your collaborators, no longer intends to obtain the list which had been requested. At all times, he reserves the right for the next year to request it prior to the beginning of the works. A special clause on this point will appear in the new authorization form which will be signed from now on by all excavators.*

3. As to the publication of accounts in the Guide—

neither your right of publication nor any customary practice in this field detracts from the right of the Egyptian Government to put on the objects displayed in the Museum (which are in the Public Domain) notices informing the public, and to publish these notices in the Museum Guide. The notices will therefore be published in the new edition of the Guide.

The decisions set out above demonstrate His Excellency's spirit of conciliation. Please note that His Excellency will not hesitate, if necessary, to enforce his decisions.

I regret that your refusal has forced us to have recourse once again to H.E. the Minister. I should, however, add that from a scientific point of view, I am in agreement with you and I cannot but approve of your methods.

The resumption of work next year will be based on a new type of contract which you as well as all your colleagues will have to sign and which will specify the rights which the Government has over the excavation sites.

It is indispensable, given the experience of the last two years, that all the disputed and any other matters be addressed in the authorizations so as to safeguard the Government's interests.

I hope never to have to exercise all the rights which we reserve to ourselves, but since there may be arguments on points which appear clear to us, it is important to make them clearer still in writing. That is the aim of the new form of authorization. The text which I have shown you is not yet finalised, but the idea is clear. As soon as possible we will communicate the final version to all our colleagues.

Please be assured, Sir, of my distinguished consideration.

Signed: THE DIRECTOR GENERAL]

This letter, which is ostensibly concerned with the questions of visitors, list of collaborators, and the proposed publication of Tut·ankh·amen material in the official Museum Guide Book, is evidently designed to force an issue which it had hitherto been
36 thought better to leave until the completion of the work, namely the exact legal position with regard to the ownership of the contents of the tomb.

The question of the ownership thus brought up could not but have a very distinct bearing on the future control of the work, and before replying to the letter Mr. Carter felt bound to take legal advice. This he did, and, though it anticipates somewhat the actual sequence of events, it will be better to give here Mr. Carter's reply.

Luxor,
February 3rd, 1924.

SIR,

I have the honour to reply to your letter of the 10th Jan., 1924, No. 27. 2/5, and I take this opportunity of replying further to your two letters of the 10th Dec., Nos. 18.14/4 and 27.2/5, and your letter of the 6th Dec., 1923, unnumbered. I note your observation: '*Le Gouvernement ne discute plus, mais vous transmet sa décision*' ['The Government refuses to discuss the issue any further, but conveys to you its decision'].

I note, with regret, that you have consulted your State Legal Department. I say with regret because it appears to me that the more dignified as well as the more prudent course would have been to postpone all disputes as to the ultimate destination of the treasures found until the continued existence of the treasures should have been secured. However, the very pointed way in which you insist that the objects found are part of the 'Public Domain,' that the rights of the Administration are 'exclusive,' and that the reservation of the rights of Almina Countess of Carnarvon is 'irrelevant,' has compelled me to turn aside from the scientific work of recording and preserving the objects, to consider, what I still regard as a matter of altogether secondary importance, the question of the legal rights to which the discovery has given rise.

I find that Law No. 14 of 1912, Article 11, provides:—

> 'Quiconque ayant découvert une antiquité mobilière, autrement qu'au cours d'une fouille illicite, se sera conforme au prescriptions de l'article précédent, recevra à titre de prime la moitié des objets trouvés ou de leur valeur.
>
> 'A défaut d'entente sur un partage amiable, le Service des Antiquités prélevera les objets qu'il entend garder.
>
> 'Pour les autres objets, le partage en deux lots d'égale valeur sera fait par le Service, et l'inventeur aura le droit de choisir entre les deux lots.
>
> 'Pour tout objet prélevé par le Service, chacune des deux parties fixera la valeur qu'elle lui attribue. Au cas ou l'inventeur n'accepterait pas la moitié fixé par le Service celui-ci aura la faculté, soit de prendre, soit d'abandonner l'objet en payant ou en recevant la moitié du prix fixé par l'inventeur lui-même.'
>
> [*Whoever discovers a portable antiquity, other than in the course of an illicit excavation, and in conformity with the preceding article, will receive the first title to one half of the objects discovered or their value.*
>
> *In the absence of an amicable division,*

> *the Antiquities Service will remove the objects which it intends to keep.*
>
> *For the other objects, the division in two lots of equal value will be made by the Service, and the finder will have the right to choose between the two lots.*
>
> *For all the objects taken by the Service, each one of the two parties will fix the value which it attributes to it. In the event that the finder does not accept the value given by the Service, it will have the right either to take or to surrender the object for payment or receive half the price fixed by the finder himself.*]

By Articles 8, 9 and 10 of the concession granted to the Earl of Carnarvon on the 18th April, 1915, and renewed each subsequent year until the death of Lord Carnarvon, April, 1923, it is provided:—

> 8. Mummies of the Kings, of Princes, and of High Priests, together with their coffins and sarcophagi, shall remain the property of the Antiquities Service,
>
> 37 9. Tombs which are discovered intact, together with all objects which they may contain, shall be handed over to the Museum whole without division.
>
> 10. In the case of tombs which have already been searched, the Antiquities Service shall, over and above the mummies and sarcophagi intended in Article 8, reserve for themselves all objects of capital importance from the point of view of history and archaeology, and shall share the remainder with the permittee.

> 'As it is probable that the majority of such tombs as may be discovered will fall within the category of the present Article, it is agreed that the permittee's share will sufficiently recompense him for the pains and labours of the undertaking.'

The tomb of Tut·ankh·amen has been searched. It was not found intact. The conclusions to be drawn from these documents appear to me to be sufficiently obvious. Until the Antiquities Department has selected the articles which it proposes to reserve, and fixed their value, until the executors of the Earl of Carnarvon have put their value on these objects, until the Antiquities Department has exercised the option of taking or leaving these objects at the last-named valuation, until the remaining articles have been divided, and until finally the executors have chosen their share, the articles found do not form part of the Public Domain, the rights of the Administration are not exclusive, and the reservation of the rights of the executors is not irrelevant.

I take this opportunity of drawing your particular attention to one reservation to which you have assented. The articles which I have already sent to the Museum were sent on the express understanding that they should form no part of the Museum collection, and were therefore, by agreement, not entered in the regular *livre d'entrée*, but in a special book provided for that purpose, so as to exclude them from the effects of the Decree of May 16th, 1883.

With regard to the work on which I am at present engaged, Article 6 of the licence already referred to provides:—

> 'The permittee or his representative, after examining the said tomb or monument, and

> having taken such notes as he may judge necessary, shall, if so desired, hand it over to the Inspector of Antiquities, or to any other agent to be appointed by the said Service'.

Consequently the exclusive right of your Department to the tomb does not commence until I have had sufficient time to examine the tomb and to take such notes as I judge necessary. As you are doubtless aware, I have so far had time to examine but a small part of the contents of the tomb, and the opportunity to examine and make notes on the rest is a fundamental right which I will not give up, and which I stand ready to protect if necessary. This right on my part appears to have been clearly recognized by yourself in July, 1923, when 'to put the matter in order' on the death of the Earl of Carnarvon you gave to Almina Countess of Carnarvon an authorization to complete the work of clearing the tomb of Tut·ankh·amen. The only
38 condition attached to the authorization referred to was that your Department reserved to itself such right of control as would enable it to avoid the criticisms made by the Press in the previous year, and to protect the workers as far as possible from unnecessary visits.

On the other hand, it was expressly recognized that the right of publication was entirely reserved for the Countess. The authorization, though expressed for the completion of the work, was limited in time till the 1st Nov., 1924. But as no authorization was necessary as far as the completion of the work in the tomb is concerned, it would be with amazement that I and the rest of the scientific world would learn that you propose to curtail the time allotted to me for the making of a record of such unparalleled importance.

At the same time I must inform you that I will not

agree to the new form of contract by which the Government reserves to itself rights which, as you assure me, it does not propose to exercise.

I shall now endeavour to make clear my reasons.

1. The Ministry claims the right to control the entry of visitors to the Tomb.

Article 2 of the concession already referred to provides:—

> 'Work shall be exercised under the control of the Antiquities Service, who shall have the right not only to supervise the work, but also to alter the manner of the execution if they so deem proper for the success of the undertaking.'

If the proposed control of visitors had anything to do with the success of the undertaking I should be the last to complain. It has not. The greater number of visitors whom I have been compelled to admit have been Press agents, and the object of their admission has been, not to ensure the success of the undertaking, but to encroach upon the right of publication which it has been admitted belongs entirely to Almina Countess of Carnarvon.

The authorization to the Countess referred to states:—

> 'The Antiquities Department reserves the right of control over the works so as to avoid the Press criticisms of last year and to protect the workers as far as possible from unnecessary visits.'

Of the visitors whom your Department has compelled me to admit there have been few, apart from the Press agents, who had any other motive than curiosity for seeking admission. Time is wasted not only on unnecessary visits, but also on fruitless discussions. Between Oct. 22nd, when I started work this season, and Dec. 17th there were fifty working days. Of these I had to spend fourteen on two journeys to Cairo for discussion, one at Gurna on discussion with yourself, and two were devoted to unnecessary visits by the Press agents. Thus a third of the time was frittered away through departmental interference, and additional demands on your part have caused further and almost equally serious interruptions to our work, from that time down to the present moment.

On the other hand, you propose that I should not admit anyone to the tomb when I am working, without a
39 permit from your Department. The suggestion that every time I wish to ask advice of experts, in any branch of the subject which the work may require, I should first have to apply to your Department for permission is, in my opinion, preposterous. It is conducive not to the success of the undertaking, but to the very opposite result.

The visitors whom I have admitted as personal friends of the expedition do not amount to a twentieth part of the total number. Moreover, they have come at our convenience and not at their convenience. They have not interfered with the work.

2. The Government claims the right to dictate to me whom I may and whom I may not employ, and insists on my submitting a list of the names of my collaborators. Again, if this claim had anything to do with the success of the undertaking I might hesitate to resist. But it has nothing to do with the success of the undertaking. The sole object is to exclude the Countess's publicity agent, and so encroach still further on the right of publication which is entirely reserved for her.

3. The Government claims the right to publish in the Museum Guide notices of the objects found in the Tut·ankh·amen tomb. This is obviously an encroachment

on the rights of the Countess, which cannot be justified by pretending that the objects described form part of the collection of the Museum, or part of the Public Domain. The articles described do not yet—and perhaps some of them never will—form part of the collection of the Museum. They only form part of the Public Domain with reservations. It is true that the publication of these notices is not a serious infringement of the rights of the Countess. If it were the only infringement it might pass unnoticed. But it does not stand alone; it is one of a series of determined efforts, connived at or instigated by the Egyptian Government, to deprive the Countess of the exclusive rights to publication which she has by custom, law, and express agreement with the Egyptian Government. Under these circumstances I will not consent to this or any other infringement.

You were good enough to state your personal feelings, and I will state mine. The work on which I am engaged has been done not for gain, but in the interest of science. The discovery of the tomb has produced great benefits for Egypt, and for the Egyptian Antiquities Department in particular. It has also produced rights in the Earl of Carnarvon, the author of these benefits. It is a matter of surprise and regret to me, that whereas every other Department of the Egyptian Government has shown only goodwill, kindness, and eagerness to help, your Department has ever since the death of the late Lord Carnarvon not only been endeavouring to frustrate the rights of the Carnarvon family, but also to impede, hinder, and delay the scientific work without which the fruits of the discovery would be wasted. I am at a loss to find the motives for this action, but I have no doubt as to what will be the verdict of the World of Science on the issue between us.

I have the honour to be, Sir,
Your obedient Servant,
Signed: HOWARD CARTER.
The Director-General, Antiquities Service,
Cairo.

40 It will readily be understood that, in view of these continual interruptions and annoyances, anything like a regular systematic piece of clearing was impossible. Nevertheless, the work advanced slowly; the shrines, with care and hard manual labour, were dismantled one by one; and the time was approaching when the sarcophagus would be bare, and it would be possible to raise its lid.

Mr. Carter had more than once, in the course of the winter, extended a cordial invitation to the Minister to be present when the ceremony should take place.

He would have been within his strict legal rights if he had insisted on carrying out the operation at his own convenience, without notifying the Government at all—there being nothing in his authorization that compelled him, the official entry into the tomb once made, to stop the work of clearing at any stage and refer it to the Department.

So far from wishing, however, to raise any objection to Government representatives being present on this occasion, it had always been his intention to notify the Department, and to request that the Minister, the Director-General of the Antiquities Service, and any other high Government officials who should so desire, should honour him by their presence.

It was with some surprise, therefore, that he received, on January 13th, the following brusque communication, which, from its tone, implied that the Government were forcing upon him a course of procedure which they were certain he would resent:—

Service des Antiquités, Le Caire,
No. 27.2/5. le 12 Janvier, 1924.

OBJET: OUVERTURE DU SARCOPHAGE DE TOUTANKHAMON

MONSIEUR,

Son Excellence le Ministre des Travaux Publics me charge de vous faire savoir que S.E. le Premier Ministre se propose de présider l'ouverture officielle du sarcophage de Toutankhamon.

Je vous prie en consequence de vouloir bien nous prévenir une semaine à l'avance de la date de l'ouverture de ce sarcophage.

Lorsque l'enlévement des sarcophages extérieurs aura progressé de façon à permettre l'ouverture de celui qui contient la momie, tout travail devra être arrêté et S.E. le Ministre des Travaux Publics prévenu aussitôt. Son Excellence tient à être présent lorsque le couvercle du dernier sarcophage sera soulevé pour la première fois. Je vous serai donc obligé de respecter ce désire et de ne pas ouvrir le sarcophage avant que Son Excellence soit présente.

Je vous prie de vouloir m'accuser réception de la présente lettre.

Veuillez agréer, Monsieur, etc.,
Pour le Directeur Général,
Signé: J. E. QUIBELL.

Monsieur Howard Carter,
Luxor.

[Antiquities Service, Cairo
No. 27.2/5. 12th January, 1924.

OBJECT: THE OPENING OF THE SARCOPHAGUS OF TOUTANKHAMON.

SIR,

His Excellency the Minister of Public Works has asked me to inform you that H.E. the Prime Minister proposes to preside over the official opening of the sarcophagus of Toutankhamon.

I should therefore be grateful if you would inform us one week in advance of the date of the opening of the sarcophagus.

When the removal of the outer coffins has proceeded to a point to allow the opening of that which contains the mummy, all work must cease and H.E. the Minister of Public Works be alerted as soon as possible. His Excellency wishes to be present when the lid of the final sarcophagus is lifted for the first time. I should therefore be grateful if you would respect this wish and not open the sarcophagus before His Excellency arrives.

Please be so kind as to acknowledge receipt of this letter.

Please be assured, Sir, etc.,

For the Director General,

Signed: J.E. QUIBELL.

Mr Howard Carter,
Luxor.]

At the same time the correspondents of the opposition Press
were continually communicating with the Minister, demanding
privileges and ventilating imaginary grievances. As a result, Mr.
41 Engelbach passed to Mr. Carter on January 13th the following
communication, which he had received from Mr. Tottenham:—

Cairo, January 12th, 1924.

ENGELBACH, Luxor.

782. Please arrange with Carter for Press to view

granite sarcophagus on fourteenth. If not possible for fourteenth without impeding Carter's work, please let me know earliest possible date with object of arranging intermediate Press visit.

TOTTENHAM.

Mr. Carter replied direct to Mr. Tottenham—

Luxor,
January 13th, 1924.

TOTTENHAM, Ashgal, Cairo.

175. Your 782. It is now physically impossible for any of us to get at or expose sarcophagus before twelve to fifteen days hence. It is my one aim to expedite this proposition, and would gladly welcome any solution which would accelerate the operation. Will communicate you few days in advance of the success of this undertaking, to enable you to make necessary arrangements. Please convey this, with my regards, to Minister.

HOWARD CARTER.

[Copy to Engelbach.]

—and received the following answer, dated January 14th, of which he sent a copy to Mr. Engelbach:—

Cairo,
January 14th, 1924.

CARTER, Luxor.

788. Your 175. Many thanks. Position clearly understood and conveyed to Minister. Am now in position to reply to protests on this subject. Please show Engelbach.

TOTTENHAM.

[Copy to Engelbach.]

A letter from Mr. Tottenham, confirming his telegram, and raising another point with regard to the communiqués to the Press, was received by Mr. Carter on Jan. 15th:—

Ministry of Public Works, Cairo.
Cairo, 15.1.1924.

DEAR CARTER,

Many thanks for your wire, which was just what I wanted. I knew perfectly well that the impossible was being asked, but the Minister was insistent on your trying to meet the protests of .... and ...., and got me to send the wire I sent to Engelbach.

You have probably heard that the communiqué is now being sent to the P.W.D. instead of the Press Bureau. The change was due to the reference to King George's wishes *re* the mummy remaining *in statu quo*. Coming as it did in a communiqué issued under Govt. auspices from Press Bureau, the native Press immediately asked if King G. or King Fuad ruled Egypt, and Abdel Hamid Pasha was criticized accordingly.

To obviate possibility of similar references appearing in future communiqués, he ordered that they pass through his hands before issue to Press; hence their dispatch to P.W.M.

42 I mention this so as, in drafting future communiqués, care may be taken not to put in anything that might cause political discussion.

What mountains are made out of molehills, eh!

Yours ever,
Signed: P. M. TOTTENHAM.

No other communications passed between the Government and Mr. Carter from the date last mentioned to that of February 4th. During this period signs were becoming increasingly evident that the Department of Antiquities was laying plans to force Mr. Carter out of the work.

M. Lacau, in conversation with a well-known archaeologist in Cairo, admitted frankly that they were intending to enforce much heavier restrictions upon Mr. Carter, and that if he refused to agree to them it was the Government's intention to cancel his authorization.

Mr. Engelbach at the same time was informing all and sundry that the Government plans for taking over the work were all prepared.

Newspaper correspondents were discussing it, and, as a cutting from the *Boston Transcript* of February 4th shows, were referring to the possibility in dispatches to their papers.

M. Lacau, if the extracts from his letters published in the Cairo papers are accurate, was at this time writing official letters to the Minister,* urging him to take strong action; and even as early as December 18th the Minister informed Mr. Carter in conversation that it had been suggested to him that the tomb be closed, but that he was unwilling to do so.

* *La Bourse Egyptienne*, 15 Février 1924.—'... En effet, au début du mois de Janvier dernier, c'est-à-dire quinze jours avant la chute du Ministère Yehia Ibrahim pasha, M. Lacau avait adressé une lettre au Ministre des Travaux Publics lui-disent que: "*D'accord avec M. Tottenham, Sous-secrétaire d'Etat aux Travaux Publics, et Abdel Hamid Badaoui bey, Conseiller Royal, il considérait que si M. Howard Carter insistait sur la question de la visite de la Tombe par ses amis, ses collaborateurs et ses connaissances, le Service des Antiquités devrait avoir la pleine liberté d'agir pour faire interdire, par la police, ces visites.*"

Bien plus.

M. Lacau fait preuve d'une grande clairvoyance et d'une grande énergie. Dans cette même lettre au Ministre des Travaux Publics, il dit:

"*...La question doit être portée devant les Tribunaux. Il y a des circonstances où la patience doit être considérée comme criminelle. C'est un coup mortel pour l'autorité gouvernementale que le Gouvernement menace toujours sans jamais se décider à l'action. Quiconque a peur de défendre ce qu'il croit être son droit s'engage dans une fausse voie pour obtenir ce droit...*"'

[La Bourse Egyptienne, *15th February 1924.—'... At the beginning of January, that is fif-*

It is interesting also in this connexion to put on record that, at the very beginning of the season, even before the work began, there was a scheme to detach the Metropolitan Museum members of Mr. Carter's staff. Tentative proposals were actually made to them, though nothing of the kind was ever intimated to Mr. Carter by the Government.

It was not until February 4th that Mr. Carter was able to bring to completion the heavy task of dismantling the shrines, and thereby render possible the raising of the lid of the stone sarcophagus. On that date he sent the following three telegrams:—

Luxor, February 4, 1924.

H.E. MORCOS BEY HANNA, Minister P.W., Cairo

186. Beg to inform Your Excellency that I was able to uncover sarcophagus yesterday, as reported in to-day's communiqué. May I suggest Your Excellency official
43 opening February twelfth? Would like to see you first. Will come Ministry Thursday if convenient. Looking forward to pleasure of meeting Your Excellency. Regards.

HOWARD CARTER.

teen days before the fall of Minister Yehia Ibrahim pasha, M. Lacau had sent a letter to the Minister of Public Works telling him that: "In agreement with Mr. Tottenham, Under-Secretary of State for Public Works, and Abdel Hamid Badaoui bey, Royal Adviser, he considered that if Mr. Howard Carter were adamant on the question of the visit to the tomb by his friends, colleagues and acquaintances, the Antiquities Service would be within its rights to have the police forbid such visits."

Even more.

M. Lacau shows evidence of his great perspicacity and vigour. In the same letter to the Minister of Public Works, he says:

"...This matter must be brought before the law courts. This is a situation where patience must be seen as a crime. It is a serious blow to governmental authority that the Government repeatedly threatens but never makes up its mind to act. Anyone who is afraid of defending that which he believes to be his right is not going the right way to enforce that right..."']

LACAU, Cairo Museum, Cairo.

Luxor, February 4, 1924.

187. Uncovered sarcophagus yesterday; have suggested official opening February twelfth.

CARTER.

TOTTENHAM, P.W., Cairo.

Luxor, February 4, 1924.

188. Uncovered sarcophagus yesterday; have suggested to Minister official opening February twelfth. Will suggest Press to view it Thursday, seventh. Will be in Cairo Thursday to see Minister.

CARTER.

In the closing days of January the Yehia Ministry had fallen, and a new one, under the premiership of Saad Pasha Zaghlool, had taken its place. It was for this reason that Mr. Carter made the suggestion in his telegram that he should call at the Ministry in order to pay his respects to the new Minister, Morcos Bey Hanna, and at the same time make arrangements for the opening of the sarcophagus.

In the telegram to Mr. Tottenham, Mr. Carter had suggested that the Press be admitted to see the sarcophagus on February 7th, rather than on the following Monday (Feb. 11th), the regular Press day. This for two reasons. He wished to comply with the Government's desire that the Press should be given an opportunity at as early a date as possible; and also because it would be absolutely necessary for him to have a free hand on February 11th, in order to make the necessary arrangements for the official opening on February 12th. As the following three documents will show, Mr. Tottenham stuck out firmly for a view on both days.

This, with a Press view after the lid was raised, would have meant no less than three such views within a period of seven days—Feb. 7th, Feb. 11th, and Feb. 13th,—and the attempt to enforce it is a commentary on the amount of interference and actual loss of time that was being imposed upon Mr. Carter.

CARTER, Luxor. Cairo, Feb. 4, 1924.

841 your 188. Agree suggestion supplementary Press view for seventh.

TOTTENHAM.

TOTTENHAM, P.W., Cairo. Luxor, Feb. 5, 1924.

189 your 841 to my 188. I mean seventh in place of eleventh, and not supplementary, so as to enable me to make preparations for opening.

CARTER.

CARTER, Luxor. Cairo, Feb. 5, 1924.

846 your 189. Have already informed all concerned that Press view on seventh will be supplementary. Could you arrange a short view on eleventh in order to avoid disappointment and criticism ?

TOTTENHAM.

In his reply from the Ministry, Mr. Carter received an appoint-
44 ment for Thursday, February 7th, and on the evening of February
6th he took train for Cairo.

HOWARD CARTER, Luxor.

Cairo, Feb. 4, 1924.

Your 186. Am charged by His Excellency the Minister to present his thanks for your telegram. He will be pleased to see you Thursday afternoon at 5 o'clock and to decide date of opening sarcophagus.

OSMAN, Secretary-General.

At 5 P.M., as arranged, Mr. Carter called on His Excellency at the Ministry. On his arrival he was informed that the Minister had been detained, and would be some twenty minutes late. While waiting he was called to see Mr. Tottenham in his office.

Mr. Tottenham advised Mr. Carter that in his interview with the Minister he should confine himself to the question of the opening of the sarcophagus. In fact, he said, it would be better if all former negotiations could be forgotten, and papers pertaining to them destroyed.

Mr. Tottenham, having thus somewhat disarmed Mr. Carter, suddenly thrust upon him a document which his Ministry considered threw light upon the division of the objects found. This document—a permit given to Mr. Carter, in the name of Lord Carnarvon, to make an investigation in another part of the Theban necropolis, where Mr. Carter thought he had made a possible discovery—will be referred to later (*see* Appendix I).

Mr. Tottenham then took Mr. Carter to the Minister's room.

The Minister received Mr. Carter cordially, but began the conversation with a complaint that he had had a visit from Dr. Alan Gardiner, supposedly sent by Mr. Carter, to protest against the treatment Mr. Carter was receiving from the Antiquities Service. To this Mr. Carter replied that he believed Dr. Gardiner's visit was actuated by the fact that he and certain other prominent archaeologists were indignant at the waste of time and danger to science that the actions of the Department were entailing on Mr. Carter's work, but that he (Mr. Carter) had had nothing to do with the visit, and had not even known that it was to take place.

The Minister then asked Mr. Carter whether he was 'd'accord' ['in agreement'] with the Antiquities Service, to which he replied that he was by no means 'd'accord' with their methods of administration, but that, apart from this, his feelings were, and always had been, quite friendly. He then asked Mr. Carter, if he should have any concrete grievance against them, to write to him on the matter; asking at the same time that on both sides bygones should be bygones.

He then stated that, though Mr. Carter might be within his legal rights, he had made a great mistake in forming a contract with *The Times*, as it had caused a nasty odour with the Press. Mr. Carter agreed, but reminded the Minister that it was not entirely his fault, since the contract had been left to him as a legacy which he had to protect. He assured the Minister, however, that after April, 1924, the contract could, and would, be brought to an end.

The Minister made a passing reference to the fact that Mr. Carter was committing a fault in going to America in the spring, on the ground that, by undertaking the work on which he was engaged, he became virtually a public servant, and should go straight on until the work was finished. This, naturally, was a point of view with which Mr. Carter could not agree.

45 Reference was then made to former negotiations, but Mr. Tottenham suggested that, as these had been of an acrimonious nature, they had better be left alone, and the Minister agreed not to bring up the past.

The conversation then turned to the arrangements for the official opening of the sarcophagus, and at this point the Minister informed Mr. Carter that M. Lacau was waiting, and suggested that he be brought into the conference.

As a commentary on the fact that both the Minister and Mr. Tottenham were insisting on a burial of the past, it should be stated that Mr. Tottenham and M. Lacau both came to the interview armed with complete dossiers, whereas Mr. Carter had brought no papers at all; and that M. Lacau's first remark to Mr. Carter was framed in the form of an accusation that he had introduced numbers of visitors into the tomb. To this Mr. Carter replied that the visitors introduced by him did not come within a twentieth part of those introduced by the Government—a statement which Tottenham assured the Minister was perfectly correct.

Mr. Carter then referred back to the main question, that of the opening of the sarcophagus, and said he hoped that he and the Prime Minister would be able to be present on that occasion. The Minister asked whether he would see 'le corps' [the body], to which Mr. Carter replied that, so far as he was able to judge from previous evidence of the customs of ancient Egyptian royal burials, he would not, but that, in all probability, the raising of the lid would disclose the outermost of a series of coffins containing the royal mummy.

The Minister showed disappointment, and said that in that case he did not consider that it would be worth while for himself and his colleagues to come. He asked why it would not be possible to open these coffins then and there, and Mr. Carter explained that this would be an incorrect scientific procedure, for that full records and photographs must be taken, a task which would require a considerable time to carry out, and which he proposed to postpone until the following season. On this point M. Lacau concurred.

Mr. Carter then made the following suggestion—that the Minister should send a delegate in his place, and that, in the presence of M. Lacau and other representatives of the Service, he would, with his collaborators, open the sarcophagus. Then, if it was agreed that the results were sufficiently interesting, advice should be given to His Excellency to come, with his colleagues, to view them. To this the Minister agreed.

Mr. Carter then requested that the regular Press visit on Monday, February 11th, should be cancelled, as there would be nothing more to be seen on that occasion than had been seen on Thursday, February 7th; and that, as the proposed opening of the Tomb was to be on February 12th, the pressmen, to enable them to see full results, should be admitted again on February 13th. After this day of the Press view, Mr. Carter requested that he might have three or four clear days, commencing from the 14th, to make his scientific records, during which no visitors should be allowed to enter the tomb. Then, after these four days, the tomb could be thrown open to visitors for a period of about ten days.

Naturally, all these arrangements of days would be dependent on the question of whether the Ministers desired to view the tomb or not. The Minister agreed to the programme, and asked Mr. Tottenham, M. Lacau and Mr. Carter to put it in writing, sign it, and present it to him. It was agreed that this should be done on the following morning (Feb. 8th), at M. Lacau's house.

46 In view of recent events, and the statement that has subsequently been made, that at this interview Mr. Carter made the request that there should be a visit of the families of his collaborators on February 13th, following the Press visit, and that the Minister definitely refused, Mr. Carter wishes to make the emphatic statement that he made no such request, and that nothing of the kind took place, the arrangements agreed upon being solely concerned with the purely official side of the programme. In confirmation of this statement, Mr. Carter would like to remind the Government that when this visit was referred to in conversation with Mohamed Pasha Zaghlool (the Minister's delegate) on the morning of February 12th, Mohamed Pasha Zaghlool expressed surprise, and said that, as this was something entirely new, he must communicate with the Minister. Mr. Carter still thinks that, out of common courtesy, he was bound to invite them, and that he was entirely within his rights, since a private visit of this sort hardly entered into the official side of the arrangements. It was, moreover, by no means an innovation, for it had been the regular procedure on all previous occasions of this kind, dictated by the common laws of politeness.

On February 8th Mr. Carter met Mr. Tottenham and M. Lacau as arranged, and in mutual agreement they framed a draft to cover the following details of official procedure:—

1. Opening of the sarcophagus.
2. Admittance of the Press.

3. Time reserved for taking records.

4. Authorized visits to the tomb.

The exact date on which the last should begin, it was agreed, should be left until it was known whether the Minister and his colleagues would enter the tomb or not. To amplify this point a fifth clause was added, in which it was agreed that, after February 13th, all visits would be suspended until the time when the tomb would be thrown open to authorized visitors.

This draft programme was signed, and given to Mr. Tottenham to convey to the Minister.

In conversation afterwards it was agreed that the authorized visitors should not exceed 750—75 a day for ten days; M. Lacau suggested 2,000—i.e. 200 per day.

Mr. Carter arrived back at Luxor on February 9th, and on the following day a new difficulty arose. Previous to his departure for Cairo, Mr. Engelbach had written him a letter, asking that a new rule be applied with regard to the question of light supplied to the tomb—namely, that if Mr. Carter wanted light in the afternoon he must give at least two hours' notice beforehand; this to enable Mr. Engelbach to check his engineer's accounts.

Mr. Carter annotated this letter, saying that frequently he could not tell until the very last moment whether he wanted the light in the afternoon or not, and suggesting that, if it was only a question of accounts, he himself would check them for him; would he, therefore, please let the arrangement of the past two seasons stand. This request was reiterated to Mr. Engelbach in conversation at the tomb.

On February 10th, Mr. Carter being very busy making arrangements for the official opening, this question of light was raised again, with the result that that afternoon his work was seriously hampered, and, as he had promised the Minister in his inter- 47
view in Cairo to let him know personally if any trouble should arise, he sent the following telegram:—

Luxor,
February 10, 1924.

H.E. MINISTER, P.W., Cairo.

Antiquity Department imposing difficulties with regard to the electric light in the tomb. Would Your Excellency instruct that light be at my disposal as hitherto.

Regards,
HOWARD CARTER.

On February 9th the subjoined letter was received from Mr. Tottenham, with two enclosures (A) and (B).

Ministry of P.W.,
Cairo.

No. C.2/1, February 10, 1924.

DEAR BETHELL,

I write to you to save time and to pass to Carter.

I enclose copy (A) of decision arrived at on Friday with Carter and Lacau. I also enclose copy (B) of Press communiqué which I hope to get published to-day (10.2.1924).

It will be noticed that the only real modification of (A) that occurs in (B) is in para. 1, where Carter's collaborators are mentioned.

When I took (A) to the Minister for confirmation, he insisted on being precise in respect of numbers and asked me to 'phone Carter to name them.

As result of lengthy discussion, in which I took up the attitude that Carter must not be interfered with, the wording was left vague in the communiqué, and Mohamed Zaghlool Pasha was instructed by H.E. the Minister to settle the number with Carter.

Zaghlool Pasha, you will find, will be quite ready to agree to anything Carter considers reasonable; and, for your information, the number it was thought Carter might require was about 10-12.

Yours sincerely,

Signed: P. W. TOTTENHAM.

A

TUT·ANKH·AMEN TOMB

OPENING OF SARCOPHAGUS AND VISITS TO VIEW

8.2.24.

The following has been decided on, 8.2.24, by Messrs. Tottenham (U.S. of State) and Lacau (D.G. of Antiquities) and Mr. Howard Carter, in accordance with the wishes of H.E. the Minister of P.W. as expressed at a meeting held in his office on 7.2.24, as follows:—

1. The opening of the sarcophagus of Tut·ankh·amen
will be carried out on 12.2.24 (Tuesday) at 3 P.M., in the
presence of a delegate of the Minister of Public Works, the
Director-General of Antiquities, the Chief Inspector of
Antiquities for Upper Egypt, the Assistant Conservateur of
the Museum (Chaban Eff.) and the Inspector of 48
Antiquities at Luxor (Ibrahim Eff.), and Mr. Carter and
his collaborators in the tomb.

2. The Press will be admitted to the tomb on the morning of 13.2.24 (Wednesday) between 10 A.M. and noon.

3. The four following days, viz. 14, 15, 16 and 17th, will be devoted to making of records by Mr. Carter and his staff, and of necessary preparations for the reception of authorized visitors.

4. Authorized visitors will be permitted to visit the tomb during ten days, commencing as soon as possible after 17.2.24 (Sunday). The actual date will depend upon

the contents of the sarcophagus, and will be announced in the Press as soon as possible.

5. With the exception of 13.2.24, which is to be devoted to the Press view, all visits will be suspended from now until the tomb is opened to authorized visitors.

Signed: P. W. TOTTENHAM,
P. LACAU, HOWARD CARTER.

B

TUT·ANKH·AMEN'S TOMB

OPENING OF SARCOPHAGUS AND VISITS TO VIEW

[*Communiqué*] 10.2.24.

The following arrangements have been decided upon by the Ministry of Public Works:—

1. The opening of the sarcophagus of Tut·ankh·amen will be carried out on 12.2.1924 (Tuesday) at 3 P.M., in the presence of the Under-Secretary of State for Public Works, the Mudir of the Province, the Director General of Antiquities, the Chief Inspector of Antiquities for Upper Egypt, the Assistant Conservateur of the Museum (Mohamed Effendi Shaban) the Inspector of Antiquities at Luxor (Ibrahim Eff. Habib) and Mr. Lucas; and Mr. Carter and those of his collaborators who are designated by the Under-Secretary of State for Public Works and Mr. Carter.

2. The Press will be admitted to the Tomb on the morning of 13.2.1924 (Wednesday) between 10 A.M. and noon.

3. The four following days, viz. 14, 15, 16 and 17th, will be devoted to the making of records by Mr. Carter and his staff, and of necessary preparations for reception of authorization visitors.

4. Authorized visitors will be permitted to visit the Tomb during ten days, commencing as soon as possible after 17.2.1924 (Sunday). The actual date will depend

upon the contents of the sarcophagus; and this, and the procedure to be adopted to obtain permits, will be announced in the Press as soon as possible.

5. With the exception of 13.2.1924, which is to be devoted to the Press view, all visits will be suspended from now until the tomb is opened to authorized visitors.

In para. 3 of his letter Mr. Tottenham remarks, 'It will be 49
noticed that the only real modification of (A) that occurs in (B) is in para. 1, where Carter's collaborators are mentioned.'

This statement is hardly accurate, for in (B) para. 1, 'the Mudir of the Province' has been added by the Government subsequently to the signing of the programme (A).

The wording of this communiqué (B), especially in para. 1, makes quite clear the exceedingly subordinate position which, in the eyes of the Government, Mr. Carter was expected to fill on this occasion, the implication being that the clearing of the tomb was a Government piece of work, and that Mr. Carter, on whom the sole responsibility and entire cost fell, was to have no say in the matter at all.

At about 5.30 P.M. on February 11th, Mr. Carter received the following document from Mohamed Pasha Zaghlool, the delegate of the Minister:—

Service des Antiquités,
Inspectorat de la Haute Egypte.
S.S. *Messir,* Luxor, 11th February, 1924.

HOWARD CARTER, ESQ., El-Qurnah.

SIR,

PROCEDURE ON THE OCCASION OF THE OPENING OF THE SARCOPHAGUS OF TUT·ANKH·AMEN ON 12TH FEBRUARY, 1924

You must have received to-day the decision of H.E.

the Minister of Public Works concerning the opening of the tomb of Tut·ankh·amen. In case there has been any delay in transmission, I send you a second copy herewith.*

I am instructed by H.E. the Minister to arrange with you the list of collaborators whom you wish to admit.

Will you, therefore, kindly send me, by to-night, your proposal for such a list.

I shall be happy to see you either to-night or to-morrow morning if such is your wish.

I have the honour to be, Sir, etc.,

U.S.S. of State, P.W.M.

Signed: M. A. ZAGHLOOL. 11.2/924.

Mr. Carter replied by note that he had had a very long and tiring day, and, for that reason, would His Excellency see him in the Valley at 11 o'clock the following morning (Feb. 12).

Accordingly, on the morning of February 12th His Excellency came to the Valley, accompanied by his secretary and by the Governor of the Province, and inspected the tomb and the arrangements Mr. Carter had made for raising the lid. There he was joined by M. Lacau, and, that the work in the tomb might not be interrupted, they proceeded to Tomb No. 15 to discuss the question of collaborators.

Mr. Carter submitted his list of collaborators, seventeen in all, and, after some discussion, these, with one exception, were agreed
50 to; the exception being Mr. Lucas, who the Under Secretary and M. Lacau insisted was a Government official, and therefore represented them and not Mr. Carter.

In subsequent conversation Mr. Carter referred to the fact that, as he had always done on these occasions, he was, as a matter of courtesy, inviting the families of his collaborators to the tomb on February 13th, after the Press view.

**See* Communiqué B.

Moh. Pasha Zaghlool, as has been already stated, expressed surprise and said that he must refer this new point to the Minister. At the time neither he nor M. Lacau raised any material objection to the plan.

The official opening took place at 3 P.M. on the same day (Feb. 12), and all provided for in the agreement were present. In addition, however, among the representatives of the Government, two minor officials, not mentioned either in conversation or in the communiqué, were introduced into the tomb. Mr. Carter noted this at the time to Mr. Bethell, who was in charge of the arrangements, and he reported it to Mr. Engelbach.

After the ceremony the whole company were entertained by Mr. Carter in the Magazine Tomb, No. 4, and the Minister's delegate, the Director of the Antiquities Service, and Mr. Carter agreed that they would be quite justified in asking the Minister and his colleagues to make a trip to Luxor to inspect the results of the afternoon's ceremony.

On the following day (Feb. 13) at 6.40 A.M. Mr. Carter received the following note:—

> DEAR MR. CARTER, S.S. *Messir,* 12.2.24.
>
> I regret to inform you that I have received a telegram from H.E. the Minister of Public Works in which he regrets that the arrangement come to with the Ministry does not permit the admission of the wives of collaborators to the tomb to-morrow, 13th February, 1924.
>
> Yours sincerely,
>
> Signed: M. A. ZAGHLOOL.

This came as a thunderclap to Mr. Carter, and he was at a loss to know what to do, the note showing him clearly enough that the Government considered he had no rights in the tomb at all.

He decided that he must go and see Mohamed Pasha

Zaghlool, the Minister's delegate, and explain to him that this action on the part of the Government was putting him in an absolutely impossible position.

Unfortunately, on his arrival at the river bank (about 10.30 A.M.) he was handed by an officer of police, before a crowd of donkey boys, dragomans, and tourists, the following two documents:—

ORDRE DE SERVICE

Son Excellence le Ministre des Travaux Publics, ayant répondu télégraphiquement qu'il regrettait de ne pouvoir autoriser la visite des femmes des collaborateurs de M. Carter pour le mercredi, 13 février, Son Excellence le Sous-
51 secretaire d'Etat vient de me transmettre l'ordre d'interdire, jusqu'à nouvel avis, l'accès de la tombe à toutes les dames qui n'ont pas réçu une Autorisation Ministérielle comme journalistes.

En conséquence, Mohamed Eff. Shaaban, Antoun Eff. Youssef et Ibrahim Eff. Habib devront interdire l'entrée de la tombe à toutes les dames qui n'ont pas une autorisation écrite.

Il va sans dire qu'ils devront exécute cette consigne avec toute la courtoisie désirable.

M. Carter a été prévenu de cette mesure.

Directeur Générale,
Service des Antiquités,
Signe: P. LACAU

Luxor, 13 Février, 1924.

As the sarcophagus lid was slowly winched up the linen-shrouded form of Tutankhamun's outermost coffin, anthropoid in form and richly gilded, came into view. Within hours of this photograph being taken, Carter and his team had downed tools in protest at the Egyptian Government's high-handed manner—the first strike in archaeological history. [Griffith Institute, Oxford]

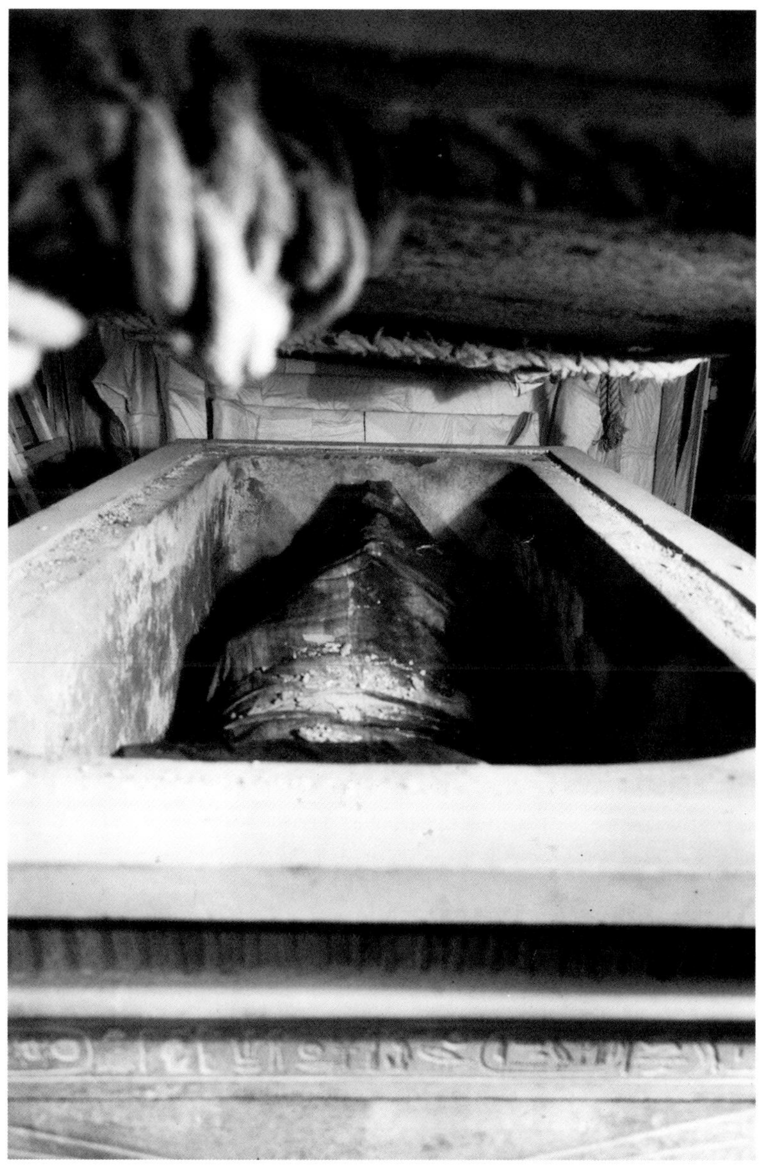

[Service Order

His Excellency the Minister of Public Works, having replied by telegram that he regrets that he is unable to authorize the visit of the wives of Mr. Carter's collaborators on Wednesday 13th February, His Excellency the Under-Secretary of State has just given the order to forbid, until further notice, access to the tomb to all ladies who have not received Ministerial Authorization as journalists.

Therefore, Mohamed Eff. Shaaban, Antoun Eff. Youssef and Ibrahim Eff. Habib must forbid entry to the tomb to all ladies who do not have written authorization.

It goes without saying that they must carry out this task with the utmost courtesy.

Mr Carter has been informed of this measure.

Director General, Antiquities Service

Luxor, 13th February, 1924. Signed: P. LACAU.]

S.S. Rakeep, Luxor, le 13 Février, 1924.

CHER M. CARTER,

Je regrette d'avoir à vous informer que je viens d'envoyer à nos agents de la Vallée des Rois l'Ordre de Service dont ci-joint copie. Ce mal entendu tardif est aussi ennuyeux pour moi* que pour vous, mais les ordres du Ministre sont formels et Son Excellence le Sous-sécretaire d'Etat me charge de vous transmettre.

Bien sincèrement votre,

Signé: P. LACAU.

[S.S. Rakeep, *Luxor, 13th February, 1924.*

DEAR MR. CARTER

I regret to inform you that I have just sent to our agents in the Valley of the Kings the Service Order of

* See footnote, page 85

which this is a copy. This belated misunderstanding is as annoying to me as it is to you, but the Minister's orders are categorical and His Excellency the Under-Secretary of State has requested that I should inform you of the same.

Most sincerely yours,

Signed: P. LACAU.]

The tone of this *Ordre de Service*, no less than its manner of delivery, made Mr. Carter realize that any further attempts at conciliation were useless.

Following on the delivery of the note, the Mamour of the Markaz (District Governor), who was on his way to the Valley on some business connected with the order, asked Mr. Carter for the loan of his car. Mr. Carter replied that as a friend he would be glad to lend it, but that he could not if the Mamour intended to take police officials with him. As the Mamour was unable to give him a straightforward answer, he sent his car away.

Mr. Carter then crossed the river, and, before seeing the Government representative, conferred with those of his collaborators who were present at Luxor. They unanimously agreed that, in face of continual interference from the Department, scientific work was becoming absolutely impossible, and that they could not continue under such conditions. Mr. Carter then went to interview the Minister's delegate on his boat, but, finding that he was away, posted the following notice in the hotel (12.30, Feb. 13):—

Luxor, Egypt.
Wednesday, February 13th, 1924.

Owing to impossible restrictions and discourtesies on the part of the Public Works Department and its Antiquity Service, all my collaborators in protest have refused to work any further upon the scientific investigations of the discovery of the tomb of Tut·ankh·amen.

I therefore am obliged to make known to the public that, immediately after the Press view of the tomb this morning, between 10 A.M. and noon, the tomb will be closed, and no further work can be carried out.

Signed: HOWARD CARTER.

52 This was a step which has been criticized in many quarters, but it must be remembered that it was absolutely necessary for Mr. Carter to take some definite action. The only alternative would have been to take some of the ladies to the tomb in the afternoon to test the carrying out of the order, but this he decided he could not do, as it would hardly have been fair to have put the ladies in such a position. After lunch, Mr. Carter sent the following telegram to the Prime Minister:—

[*Telegram*]

H.E. ZAGHLOOL PASHA, Luxor, February 13, 1924.
Prime Minister, Cairo.

I beg to call Your Excellency's attention to a gross insult I have received from officials Antiquities Service, preventing me to-day taking members of families of my collaborators to visit Tut·ankh·amen's Tomb. Feel sure Your Excellency would disapprove of this ungentlemanly action which is also illegal and unjustifiable. As a result my colleagues have protested and refused further work on this scientific investigation. I regret I am thus forced to close tomb and take action against Egyptian Government.

HOWARD CARTER.

He then made a second call on Mohamed Pasha Zaghlool, expressed his astonishment and resentment at what had happened, and left at once. The documents following on the events of this day speak for themselves:—

[*Telegram*] Cairo, Feb. 14, 1924.
HOWARD CARTER, Luxor.

Réponse à votre télégramme du 13 courant, le refus opposé a votre demande de faire visiter par des familles le tombeau le jour réservé à la Presse est basé sur un accord antérieur auquel vous avez participé. Les fonctionnaires des Antiquités n'ont fait qu'exécuter les instructions que leur avaient été donnés. On ne saurait donc les blâmer en aucune manière. Libre à vous actionner le Gouvernement, mais celui-ci entend que les dates pour les visites soient respectées.

Quant à fermer la tombe comme vous le dites, il m'est possible d'avoir à vous rappeler qu'elle n'est pas votre proprieté. La science dont vous vous acclamez à juste titre ne peut admettre que sur un incidente de visite de particuliers que vous voulez privilégier vous abandonniez vos collègues et vous les investigations auxquelles s'intéressent à un si haut point non seulement l'Egypte mais le monde entier.

ZAGHLOOL.

[Telegram *Cairo, Feb. 14th, 1924.*
HOWARD CARTER, Luxor.

In response to your telegram of the 13th inst., the refusal of your demand for a visit to the tomb by the families on the day reserved for the Press is based on an earlier agreement in which you participated. The agents of the Antiquities Service have done no more than carry out their orders. They are not to be blamed in any way. You are free to sue the Government, but the dates for visits must be respected.

As for closing the tomb as you threaten, I could respond that it is not your property. The science which you rightly invoke cannot allow that, for a private view-

ing which you would like to take place, you and your colleagues should abandon the investigations which are of a superior interest not only to Egypt but to the whole world.
ZAGHLOOL.]

February 15, 1924 (11.45 p.m.).

Having read in the daily Press that I should be refused admission to the tomb of Tut·ankh·amen, and desiring to verify the statement and also to satisfy myself as to the state of the locks on the two tombs and magazines, I went to the Valley accompanied by my friend Mr. H. E. Winlock.

On arriving, I met the Mamour and exchanged greetings with him. I then examined the locks on the outer wooden door of the tomb and on the steel gate of No. 15 (laboratory). On returning from No. 15, I met Ibraham Effendi Habib, who volunteered the information that he
53 was there to guard the tomb and the laboratory. When I asked him what he was to guard against, he replied against my entering the tomb or anyone else, 'even one of us,' until further orders. When I asked him under what authority he was acting, he voluntarily produced an Ordre de Service (attached herewith, a copy afterwards sent to me by the Chief Inspector of Antiquities) which he assured me he intended to enforce.

I asked if I might have a copy of this order, since I was ignorant of it. Ibrahim Effendi replied that he was unable to give me a copy without the permission of the Chief Inspector, and he telephoned at once for such permission. The Chief Inspector was not at his house.

I inquired from Ibrahim Effendi when the order was given out. He replied that it was given to the inspector on duty in the Valley on Wednesday (Feb. 13, 1924), he (Ibrahim) being elsewhere.

This is an exact account of what took place and has been verified by Mr. Winlock.

THE IRON GATE FITTED BY CARTER TO SAFEGUARD THE TOMB'S TREASURES FROM THEFT. AS THOMAS HOVING, A RECENT COMMENTATOR ON THE DEVELOPING CRISIS, OBSERVED, ITS PRESENCE SOON BECAME 'A MALEVOLENT SYMBOL OF FOREIGN SUPREMACY' [HOVING, *TUTANKHAMUN. THE UNTOLD STORY*, P. 159], AS MUCH TO KEEP THE EGYPTIANS OUT AS THE GOLD IN. [GRIFFITH INSTITUTE, OXFORD]

Form No. 952 F.C.
No. 1/15.2CF.

Service des Antiquités,
Inspectorat de la Haute Egypte,
Luxor,
15 February, 1924.

HOWARD CARTER, ESQ.
DEAR SIR,

In reply to your request that you be furnished with the text of the Ordre de Service *re* the closing of the Tomb of Tutankhamen and repair tomb, I beg to inform you that the terms are as follows:—

ORDRE DE SERVICE

Issued by P. Lacau, Directeur Générale of the Antiquities Department, at the order of the Under-Secretary of State, P.W.D., on board S.S. *Messir,* about 5.45 P.M. on 13 Feb., 1924 (issued to those concerned at the tomb on morning of 14 Feb.).

1. La tombe est fermée jusqu'à nouvel ordre. Personne, ni M. Carter, ni ses collaborateurs, ni le personnel du Service des Antiquités, ne peuvent y entrer.

2. Un des trois agents du Service sera toujours de garde—Mohamed Eff. Chaaban, Ibrahim Eff. Habib, et Antoun Youssef partageront le travail de façon que, jour et nuit, l'un d'eux soit de service. Ils empêcheront d'entrer dans le tombeau et dans le tombe No. 15 servant comme laboratoire.

3. Trois ghafirs seront toujours de garde avec l'un d'eux.

4. S'il se produit quelque chose d'anormal, l'inspecteur de Service avertira l'officier de police de Service et préviendra par téléphone le Mamour de Louxor, qui avertira le Moudir de Keneh et l'Inspecteur en chef.

5. L'Inspecteur en chef sera chargé de cette mesure.

[Service Order

Issued by P. Lacau, Director General of the Antiquities Department, at the order of the Under-Secretary of State, P.W.D., on board S.S. Messir, *about 5.45 P.M. on 13 Feb., 1924 (issued to those concerned at the tomb on morning of 14 Feb.).*

1. The tomb is closed until further notice. No one, not Mr. Carter, not his collaborators, not the personnel of the Antiquities Service, is permitted to enter.

2. One of the three agents of the Service shall always be on guard—Mohammed Eff. Chaaban, Ibrahim Eff. Habib, and Antoun Youssef shall share the work so that, day and night, one of them is always on duty. They will prevent entry to the tomb and tomb no. 15 which is being used as a laboratory.

3. Three ghafirs will be on guard with each of them.

4. If something abnormal occurs, the inspector of the Service will warn the police officer of the Service and notify by telephone the Mamour of Luxor, who will alert the Moudir of Keneh and the Chief Inspector.

5. The Chief Inspector will be charged with this measure.]

I assume that, when you shut down work in the tombs 54
on the morning of the 13 Feb., you took out all the personal and private property of yourself and your collaborators. If this is not the case, will you please communicate either with me or direct to Cairo, so that this matter may be examined and regulated.*

* In view of the fact that the elaborate scaffolding and machinery, the packing material, the wooden cases, etc., and even the steel and wood gates themselves—in fact, the entire working apparatus of two seasons—all belonged to the expedition, such a statement is futile in the extreme.

Faithfully yours,

Signed: REX ENGELBACH,

Chief Inspector, Upper Egypt.

[*Telegram*] Luxor, February 17th, 1924.

To H.E. Minister Public Works Department, Cairo.

201. Last Friday I was excluded from Tut·ankh·amen Tomb by armed police. I was shown Service Order of Director-General Antiquities that I was to be excluded till further orders. To-day no further orders have been given, and I was again excluded. I regard action of Director-General Antiquities as both insulting and illegal. It is essential to ensure the safety of sarcophagus and contents that I should be granted access, to which I am entitled because the arrangements made last Monday for suspending the sarcophagus cover were only intended to be temporary. Moreover, I must be given opportunity to take full precautions for safe-guarding contents of tomb and laboratory during period of cessation of work. Will Your Excellency please reply immediately, as matter could not be more urgent.

HOWARD CARTER.

[*Telegram*]

MR. HOWARD CARTER, Luxor.

Cairo, Feb. 18, 1924.

Votre dépêche no. 201 d'hier. Je regrette de vous dire que les mesures dont vous vous plaignez n'ont été prise par les autorités locales qu'après que vous-même avez fermé le tombeau en contravention du programme convenue entre vous et le Ministre, et que vous et vos collaborateurs vous êtes mis en grève, et enfin après que vous avez publié le 13 courant par voie d'affichage qu'aucun travail ultérior ne serait exécuté. Je suis même profondément étonné d'apprendre que lorsque vous avez fermé le tombeau vous n'ayez pas pris toutes les précautions nécessaires en vue d'assurer la securité du sarcophage qui intéresse tant la science et le monde entier. Je fais toutes mes réserves en cas de dommages. Toutefois afin de vous donner une dernière chance je vous invite à exécuter les obligations qui vous incombent en tant que représentant de la bénéficiaire de l'autorisation. Si par conséquent vous ne m'informez pas dans les quarante-huit heures et par écrit que vous êtes prêt à reprendre l'exécution du programme convenue le huit courant, l'autorisation de fouilles sera immédiatement annulée. Les fonctionnaires du Service des Antiquités ont reçu des instructions pour être présents et vous assister dans le cas de reprise de travaux en exécution du programme.

Le Ministre des Travaux Publics,

MORCOS HANNA.

[Telegram

MR. HOWARD CARTER, Luxor.

Cairo, Feb. 18th, 1924.

Your telegram no. 201 of yesterday. I regret to inform you that the measures of which you complain were taken by the local authorities only after you yourself closed the tomb in contravention of the plan agreed between you and the Minister, and after you and your collaborators went on strike, and finally after you made public on 13th inst. by means of a notice that no more work would be carried out. I am also very surprised to learn that when you closed the tomb you did not take all necessary precautions to ensure the safety of the sarcophagus which is of such interest to science and the whole world. I make clear all my reservations in case of possible damage. However, in order to give you one last chance, I invite you to carry out the obligations which are incumbent upon you as the representative of the holder of the authorization. If you do not inform me within forty-eight hours and in writing that you are ready to return to carrying out the plan agreed the eighth inst., the excavation authorization will be immediately revoked. The agents of the Antiquities Service have been instructed to be present and to assist you in restarting the process of carrying out the programme.

The Minister of Public Works,

MORCOS HANNA.]

55 [*Telegram*] Luxor, Feb. 19, 1924.

H.E. Minister Public Works Department, Cairo.

206. In order to safeguard the contents of the tomb I am commencing proceedings in the Mixed Courts to-day. If Director-General Antiquities will apologize for his insult to the ladies invited by myself on behalf of Almina Countess Carnarvon to the tomb on Wednesday last, when the tomb was free from the Press visit, and if an undertaking is given that all vexatious interference will cease, I will reopen the tomb for ten days in accordance with the agreement of February eighth, of which you have broken Art. three,

HOWARD CARTER.

Mr. Carter then wrote to Mr. F. M. Maxwell, his lawyer, as follows:—

Luxor, February 18, 1924.

DEAR MAXWELL,

In accordance with your wish, conveyed to me by Merton, I send you herewith the note of the measures I want to take to safeguard the objects in the Tut•ankh•amen Tomb and the laboratory tomb:

TUT•ANKH•AMEN TOMB

1. Lowering the lid on to the sarcophagus.

2. Collecting our private scientific notes.

3. Affixing water-tight door to the entrance of passage.

4. Covering entrance within the retaining walls with adequate amount of debris to prevent any possibility of tampering, theft or burglary.

LABORATORY TOMB

1. Protecting certain objects under treatment when the tomb was closed.

2. Placing within laboratory sections of pall now outside.

3. Removing card index of the record of the work, which is private property.

4. Closing its steel gate and battening it for safety, as was done at the close of last season.

5. Arranging with the Government officials for the transport to Cairo of six large cases of antiquities which are too large to be placed in the laboratory, and are thus lying outside entrance of ditto.

Over and above these items which concern the tomb and the laboratory, I naturally wish to put all my private property, now lying in various parts of the Valley, in a position of security, as has been customary heretofore.

The measures of security could be carried out in three days, but it would be better for all concerned that I have at least four.

I should note that at the present moment the Government have not interfered with me in regard to the material lying in the Valley, nor with regard to the tombs lent me for purpose of dark-room and store. Of course, as last summer, I shall expect again to be allowed to leave at least three of my men on duty in the Valley as gaffirs for my side.

Yours sincerely,
Signed: HOWARD CARTER.

56 [*Telegram*]
HOWARD CARTER, Louxor. Cairo Feb. 20, 1924.

J'ai l'honneur de vous transmettre le texte de l'Arrêté Ministériel que S.E. le Ministre des Travaux Publics vient de signer aujourd'hui et qu'il m'a chargé d'exécuter.

LACAU.

[*Telegram*
HOWARD CARTER, Luxor. Cairo Feb. 20th, 1924.

I have the honour to send you the text of the Ministerial ruling which H.E. the Minister of Public Works has just signed today and which he has charged me with executing. LACAU.]

Le Ministre des Travaux Publics. Vu les autorisations de fouilles accordées à Lord Carnarvon en 1915 et 1918, et celle accordée à Lady Carnarvon en 1923 pour continuer le déblaiement de la Tombe de Tout·ankh·amen dans la Vallée des Rois à Louxor: Vu le programme des travaux, annotations et visites arrêté le 8 Février, 1924, après la découverte du sarcophage royal suivant accord entre le Ministre des Travaux Publics et Mr. Carter representant de Lady Carnarvon et chargé par elle de la direction du chantier des fouilles: Considérant que le jour du 13 Février, le lendemain de l'ouverture du sarcophage, Mr. Carter a interrompu l'exécution du programme convenu en fermant le tombeau et en déclarant publiquement qu'aucun travail ultérieur ne serait plus exécuté: Qu'invité formellement le 18 Février suivant à reprendre l'exécution du programme convenu, il a decliné d'obtempérer à cette invitation en posant pour la réouverture du tombeau des conditions injustifiées et inacceptables pour le Gouvernement: Considérant que cette fermeture et cet abandon du travail constituent une infraction grave aux obligations assumées par lui: Que cette infraction est d'autant plus grave que de son propre-aveu elle expose les précieuses antiquités découvertes à les dommages irréparables: Considérant qu'aux termes de l'Art. 13 de l'autorisation de 1915 toute infraction de la part du permissionnaire ou ses agents aux conditions de l'autorisation entraîne de pleine droit sans aucun avis ni formalité quelconque l'annulation de l'autorisation: Que cette mesure s'impose d'autant plus que depuis le renouvellement de l'autorisation accordée à Lady Carnarvon, Mr. Carter a constamment méconnu l'autorité et le droit de contrôle du Service des Antiquités et que par sa lettre du 3 Février, 1924, qu'il a publiée il a ouvertement dénié les droits de l'Etat sur les antiquités découvertes: Pour ces motifs et sur la proposition du Directeur Générale du Service des Antiquités—

ARRÊTÉ

Article 1er. L'autorisation de fouilles accordée à Lady Carnarvon le 12 Juillet, 1923, et venant à expiration le 24 Novembre, 1924, est annulée.

Article 2. Le Directeur Générale du Service des Antiquités est chargé de l'exécution du présent arrêté. Il procédera immediatement à l'ouverture de la tombe et des laboratoires et autres dépôts, et prendra d'urgence toutes les mesures nécessaires pour la sauvegarde et la conservation de toutes les antiquités qui s'y trouvent.

Signé: MORCOS HANNA.

[*The Minister of Public Works. Considering the excavation authorizations granted to Lord Carnarvon in 1915 and 1918, and the authorization granted to Lady Carnarvon in 1923 to continue the clearing of the Tomb of Tout•ankh•Amen in the Valley of the Kings at Luxor: Considering the programme of works, notes and visits decided upon on the 8th February, 1924, after the discovery of the royal sarcophagus following the agreement between the Minister of Public Works and Mr. Carter representing Lady Carnarvon and charged by her with the direction of the excavation works: Considering that on the 13th February, the day after the opening of the sarcophagus, Mr. Carter interrupted the work on the programme agreed upon by closing the tomb and declaring publicly that no further work would be carried out: That when formally invited on the 18th February following to restart the work on the agreed programme, he declined to do so by placing unjustified and unacceptable conditions on the Government for the reopening of the tomb: Considering that this closure and this abandonment of work constitutes a serious offence especially as it exposes the precious antiquities discovered to irreparable damage: Considering the terms of Art. 13 of the authorization of 1915 any breach on the part of the holder of the authorization or his agents to the conditions triggers without warning the cancellation of the authorization: That this measure is even more justified considering that since the renewal of the authorization granted to Lady Carnarvon, Mr. Carter has constantly ignored the Antiquities Service's authority and right of control and that by his letter of the 3rd February, 1924, that he published, he has openly denied the rights of the State over the antiquities discovered: For these reasons and on the proposal of the Director General of the Antiquities Service—*

RULING

Article 1. The authorization to excavate granted to Lady Carnarvon on the 12th July, 1923, and expiring the 24th November, 1924, is cancelled.

Article 2. The Director General of the Antiquities Service is charged with the enforcement of the present ruling. He will proceed immediately to the opening of the tomb and the laboratories and other store-rooms, and will with urgency take all measures necessary to safeguard and conserve all the antiquities found there.

Signed: MORCOS HANNA.]

[*Telegram*]
HOWARD CARTER, Louxor. Cairo, 21 Feb., 1924.

Comme suite à mon télégramme du 20 Février et à ma
lettre de ce jour qui le confirm, je vous informe que je pars
ce soir pour procéder à l'ouverture de la tombe conformément à l'Arrêté Ministériel du 20 courant. Je serais 57
heureux que vous soyez présent avec vos collaborateurs à
cette opération. Je recevrai avec plaisir toutes les indica-
tions et suggestions que vous croirez devoir me faire à ce
propos. Je serai à la Vallée de Rois devant le tombeau
demain vendredi à deux heures de l'après-midi, 22 Février.

LACAU.

[*Telegram*
HOWARD CARTER, Luxor. Cairo, 21st Feb., 1924.

Following my telegram of 20th February and my letter of the same day which confirms it, I inform you that I will leave this evening to proceed with the opening of the tomb by virtue of the Ministerial Ruling of 20th inst. I will be happy for you to be present with your collaborators during this operation. I will be pleased to receive from you all information and suggestions that you consider necessary on this matter. I will be at the Valley of the Kings in front of the tomb tomorrow, Friday, at 2 P.M., 22nd February.

LACAU.]

S.S. *Rakeeb*, Louxor, le 22 Février, 1924.

MONSIEUR CARTER,

Comme ma dépêche d'hier et ma lettre de ce matin vous l'ont appris l'autorisation de fouilles accordée à Lady Carnarvon ayant été annulée, je dois en conséquence prendre possession de la tombe cette après-midi. Comme je vous l'ai déjà dit, j'estime très utile que cette opération soit faite en votre présence, ou avec le concours de vos collaborateurs. Il faut que nous puissions convenir des mesures les plus convenables pour la sauveguarde des objets pendant tout l'été, le travail devant demeurer suspendu pendant l'action judicière. Je désirerais donc vous parler le plus tôt possible de ce qu'il convient de faire. Je vous avais fixé rendez-vous à deux heures devant la tombe. Voulez-vous que je m'arrêté plutôt à deux heures chez vous? Je préférerais vous entretenir en dehors du public. Nous pourrions ensuite aller ensemble vers trois heures à la tombe.

Voudriez vous me répondre par le porteur sur le bateau *Rakeeb*.

Voudrez vous croire, M. Carter, etc.,

Signé: P. LACAU,

Directeur Générale du Service des Antiquités.

[S.S. Rakeeb, *Luxor, 22nd February, 1924.*

MR CARTER,

As per my telegram of yesterday and my letter of this morning which notified you that the excavation authorization accorded to Lady Carnarvon had been cancelled, I must therefore take possession of the tomb this afternoon. As I have already told you, I deem it useful that this operation should take place in your presence, or with the co-operation of your collaborators. As the work must be suspended during the judicial action, we must try to agree the most appropriate measures to safeguard the objects during the entire summer. I would like, therefore, to speak to you as soon as possible about what needs to be done. I had arranged to meet you at 2 P.M. in front of the tomb. Would you like me instead to stop at your house at 2 P.M.? I would prefer to talk to you out of the public eye. We could then go together around 3 P.M. to the tomb.

Would you reply via the porter on the boat Rakeeb.

Believe me, Mr Carter, etc.,

Signed: P. LACAU,

Director General of Antiquities.]

Luxor,

February 22nd, 1924.

MONSIEUR LACAU,

In reply to your letter just received by messenger (11.30 A.M.), I would like to point out that you forcibly took possession of the tomb on February 13th, and stationed an armed guard to prevent my entering it. This being the case, and in view of the fact that the question of sequestratorship of the tomb is to come up in the Courts to-morrow, February 23rd, I fail to see why you find it necessary to force an entrance into the tomb to-day.

I would suggest that, as there is no immediate danger, it will be the more fitting time to consider the measures that must be taken to safeguard the tomb and its contents during 'l'action judicière' [the judicial action] after the Court has made its decision.

Believe me, Monsieur Lacau,
Yours faithfully,
Signed: HOWARD CARTER.

S.S. *Rakeeb,* Louxor, le 22 Février, 1924 (1h. P.M.).
MONSIEUR CARTER,

Je reçois a l'instant votre réponse (lh. P.M.). Les ordres que j'ai reçu sont formels; je dois ouvrir la tombe aujourd'hui même en exécution de l'Arrêté Ministériel. Cette mesure est indépendante de l'action legale, et elle resulte administrativement du fait que l'autorisation est annulée.

58 Puisque l'ouverture ne peut être remise et que je dois la faire avec vous ou sans vous, je vous pris de me remettre les clefs ou de m'accompagner à la tombe.

Si je n'ai pas les clefs à deux heures et demie à la tombe, j'aurai le regret d'exécuter sans vous l'ordre que j'ai reçu.

Voudrez vous croire, etc.,
Signé: P. LACAU.

[S.S. Rakeeb, *Luxor, 22nd February, 1924 (1 P.M.).*
MR CARTER,

I have just received your reply (1 P.M.). The orders that I have received are clear: I must open the tomb today in execution of the Ministerial Ruling. This measure is independent of any legal action, and is an administrative one resulting from the cancellation of the authorization.

Since the opening cannot be put off and I must do it with or without you, I request you to send me the keys or accompany me to the tomb.

If I do not have the keys at half past two at the tomb, I regret that I will have to carry out my orders without you.

Believe me, etc,

Signed: P. LACAU.]

Luxor, February 22, '24.

SIR,

With reference to your request for the keys of Tut•ankh•amen's Tomb and those of the Laboratory (Tomb No. 15).

I regret to inform you that as the matter in dispute has been referred to the Mixed Courts, and the hearing of the same has been fixed for Saturday, February 23, at 10 A.M., it would be wrong on my part to hand over the keys to anyone until instructions have been received in accordance with this finding.

I am, Sir,

Yours faithfully,

Signed: HOWARD CARTER.

The Director-General, Antiquities Service.

I must herewith enter a formal protest against the opening of the tomb, and beg that you will do no damage either to the tomb or private property.

Signed: H. C.

2.15 P.M. of same date.

[*Telegram*] Feb. 22, 1924.

MAXWELL, c.o. Cateaux, Gresham House,
Soliman Pasha Street, Cairo.

214. Doors of Tomb and Laboratory forced open this afternoon by Government officials. I protested in writing against such action, but of no avail. CARTER.

Monsieur Lacau and a number of other officials, including the Chief Inspector, Mr. Engelbach, with an armed force comprising foot police, mounted police, and camel corps, proceeded up the Valley about 2.15 P.M., forced open the doors of the Tomb of Tut·ankh·amen and the door of the Laboratory, No. 15. They left the Valley about 6 P.M. Some of my material (private property) was taken and used for some purpose inside the King's Tomb. My Egyptian staff, comprising four reises, safeguarding my private belongings in the Valley, were ordered to take their bedding and leave the Valley.

Signed: HOWARD CARTER.

February 22, 1924.

With reference to the proceedings in the Valley of February 22nd, P.M., Mr. Carter's reis, Ahmed Gerigar, states as follows:—

59 M. Lacau, Mr. Engelbach, M. Baraize, Chaban Eff., Ibrahim Eff., the Sheikh of the Antiquity guards, and their smith, arrived in the Valley accompanied by the Governor of the Province, the Commandant of the Police, the Mamour and Molais of Merqis Luxor, and thirty-three armed police—camel- and horse-mounted and foot. There was also another Government representative(?) of judicial side.* They proceeded to cut the padlocks on the steel gates of both the tomb and the laboratory. Entered therein. Made a 'procès-verbal' [written statement] and made certain dispositions within the tomb, using material belonging to the expedition both within and without the tomb. The Antiquity officials ordered me and my three assistants to leave our respective posts. We were prevented

*Mohamed Riad Bey, Director of the Legal Department, P.W.M.

guarding even the photographic laboratory, so we retired to the magazine, where we were left unhindered. I understand they are continuing their procedure in the laboratory to-day.

60

SUMMARY

THE main causes which have led up to the present unfortunate deadlock are three:—

1. *The Times* contract.

2. Monsieur Lacau's unnecessary interference in departmental matters with regard to the tomb.

3. The question of the division of the objects found.

1. The contract with *The Times* was made originally by Lord Carnarvon, and carried out subsequently by Mr. Carter, as a means of escape from an absolutely impossible situation.

So great and far-reaching was the excitement caused by the first news of the discovery, that it became evident, almost at once, that to avoid constant interruption, and consequent danger to the work, some means must be found of issuing news to the world's Press through a single organization.

The contract was not a money-making proposition on either side, for the transaction represented a monetary loss as far as *The Times* was concerned, and the money received by the expedition was all devoted to the very heavy expenses of the work.

It is difficult to see what reasonable objection could be raised to the scheme, yet certain journals in England set themselves to oppose it tooth and nail, and their correspondents—who were themselves, be it noted, endeavouring to secure exclusive rights for themselves at the time *The Times* contract was signed—inaugurated a campaign of slander and abuse that overstepped all bounds.

Had these correspondents confined their activities to their dispatches for home consumption no harm would have been done, for, in the long run, the violence of their language merely brought discredit on themselves. Unfortunately, however, not content with trying to make mischief at home, they set themselves to stir up trouble in Egypt, and this at a time when delicate negotiations were proceeding between the two countries and it was exceedingly important that no incidents should occur.

In *The Times* contract the Egyptian Press were specially considered. It was expressly stated that they should be supplied with news free of all charge, and arrangements were made by which they should get the news in time to publish it simultaneously with the London papers. The best commentary on this side of the situation is the fact that by the end of last season, with two exceptions—one European and one Egyptian—the Egyptian papers had all accepted *The Times* service.

Again, this year, there was no reason for any trouble. Mr.
Carter had arranged to transmit the news to Cairo in time for the
daily issue at his own expense—an arrangement which Mr.
Quibell, of the Antiquities Service, characterized as most generous.
He had further arranged with *The Times* that Mr. Merton should 61
be relieved of all other work and definitely attached to his staff. All
dispatches were to be sent in Mr. Carter's name.

Everything went well until the representatives of the opposition press appeared upon the scene once more. As in the previous year, they tried to break *The Times* contract by negotiating for a daily evening bulletin to be issued to all correspondents. Failing in this, they made Mr. Merton's presence on the work the pretext for an attack, on the ground that this constituted a grave infringement of the rights of the Egyptian people.

Had the Government stood firm the clamour would soon have abated. Instead, they allowed themselves to be influenced by foreign pressmen, who were actuated solely by pique, and as a result we find the Department of Antiquities, directed by archaeologists, playing into the hands of journalists, whose sole purpose was to make mischief, and not only not protecting, but actually even hindering, fellow archaeologists, who, as the Department itself admitted, were carrying out a very difficult piece of scientific work in a manner that could not be bettered.

2. It is generally agreed among archaeologists who work in the country that M. Lacau's methods of administration are a menace to the whole future of archaeology in Egypt.

The new laws he has been trying to bring into operation during the past two years would infallibly put a premium on unscientific digging, and would result in driving out of the country certain expeditions, which would refuse to work other than conscientiously, and yet could not afford to do so under the new laws.

His administration with regard to excavations is needlessly autocratic, his attitude being concisely stated in his own words, 'the excavator has no rights'.

This being his general attitude, his actions with regard to the present tomb are comprehensible enough. Here was a discovery, the greatest that Egypt or any other country had ever known, and the control of the work was, by his concession, left almost entirely in the hands of the excavator. Here, in M. Lacau's eyes, was a clear case for Government intervention. The concessionnaire must either submit to complete Government control of the work, or he must surrender his rights under the concession, and allow the Government to take the find from him altogether.

The first alternative was obviously impossible when dealing with a man who had any self-respect whatever; the second, if we may judge from the Government attitude throughout the past season, was what M. Lacau intended to bring about.

The policy of constant interferences and attempted restrictions can hardly be explained otherwise, though as a matter of fact it needs no explanation at all, for we know, from evidence in the dossier, that M. Lacau had his plans for taking over the tomb already tabulated, and even as early as December was urging the Minister to take the decisive step.

'Le Gouvernement ne discute plus, il transmet sa décision' ['The Government refuses to discuss the issue any further, but conveys to you its decision']. These are hardly the words to use to one

who is expending his whole energy on the work, who is defraying its entire cost, and who, by general consent, in the scientific carrying out of that work is beyond reproach.

3. The question of ownership of the objects is one which Mr. Carter would much rather have left until the work in the tomb was
finished. Undoubtedly, by the terms of the concession, Lord 62
Carnarvon's executors had a legal claim to some part of the find, but, in comparison with the necessity of correct scientific procedure in salvaging the contents of the tomb, it was a point of little importance, at any rate for the moment, and could have been kept out of the arena.

The Government, on the other hand, were evidently much exercised by this question, and lost no opportunity of putting it on record that they considered that the find, absolutely and entirely, was government property.

This forced the question into the open, and Mr. Carter was bound to register a protest. Had he refrained from doing so, the Government would have insisted that by tacit consent he admitted their claim—an admission which would have given the Government an even stronger pretext for assuming complete control of the work.

These were the main causes of the trouble. There were other minor ones arising from them which show up clearly enough in the documents.

Clear, too, from the documents are the increasing acrimony with which the Government dealt with the situation, and the entire absence of appreciation of the great benefit which the country in general, and the Department in particular, were deriving from Mr. Carter's work. Mr. Carter was to be forced to surrender his independence altogether, and to become, for the time being, a servant of the Department.

Submission to the Government's demands would have meant that Mr. Carter would have had to carry out his work under the following conditions:—

(1) He, as representative of Almina Countess of Carnarvon, was to do the actual work himself and to be responsible for any accident or damage that might occur, but the Department was to have absolute powers of control over the operations, and the right to interfere in any way and at any moment they pleased.

(2) He was to bear the entire cost of the work, and to receive no recompense whatever.

(3) He was to admit to the tomb any visitor whom the Government might choose to send, and at the same time must not admit a personal friend, or even a visiting archaeologist, without first asking the Government's permission.

(4) He must submit a list of his collaborators to the Government, that they might strike out any name they pleased.

(5) He must agree to the presence of three Egyptian inspectors on his work, to prevent his stealing objects.

(6) He must give the Government the right to publish anything they pleased about his work.

The insulting Ordre de Service [Service Order] already referred to was the culmination of a series of groundless inferences and slights which the Government had imposed upon Mr. Carter, and we leave the reader to judge whether it was an insult which a man with any atom of self-respect could submit to.

63 ORDRE DE SERVICE

> Son Excellence le Ministre des Travaux Publics ayant répondu télégraphiquement qu'il regrettait de ne pouvoir autoriser la visite des femmes des collaborateurs de M. Carter pour le mercredi, 13 Février, Son Excellence le Sous-secrétaire d'Etat vient de me transmettre l'ordre d'in-

terdire jusqu'à nouvel avis l'accès de la tombe à toutes les dames qui n'ont pas reçu une Autorisation Ministérielle comme journalistes.

En conséquence, Mohamed Eff. Shaban, Antoun Eff. Youssef, et Ibrahim Eff. Habib devront interdire l'entrée de la tombe à toutes les dames qui n'ont pas une autorisation écrite.

Il va sans dire qu'ils devront exécuter cette consigne avec toute la courtoisie désirable.

M. Carter a été prévenu de cette mesure.

Directeur Général,
Service des Antiquités,
Signé: P. LACAU.

Luxor, 13 Février, 1924.

[*Service Order*

His Excellency the Minister of Public Works, having replied by telegram that he regrets that he is unable to authorize the visit of the wives of Mr. Carter's collaborators on Wednesday 13th February, His Excellency the Under-Secretary of State has just given the order to forbid, until further notice, access to the tomb to all ladies who have not received Ministerial Authorization as journalists.

Therefore, Mohamed Eff. Shaaban, Antoun Eff. Youssef and Ibrahim Eff. Habib must forbid entry to the tomb to all ladies who do not have written authorization.

It goes without saying that they must carry out this task with the utmost courtesy.

Mr Carter has been informed of this measure.

Director General,
Antiquities Service
Signed: P. LACAU.

Luxor, 13th February, 1924.]

64

APPENDIX I

Re permit to make an investigation in another part of the Theban Necropolis—having no relation to the Valley of the Kings.

To the Director, Luxor, Nov. 21, 1918.
Service des Antiquités, Cairo.

DEAR SIR,

Re our conversation in Cairo in regard to my possible discovery of an isolated tomb, far away from the Theban Necropolis, hidden in a very remote spot in the cliffs of the great Northern Valley—N. of the Valley of the Kings—

Would you kindly grant me a temporary authorization to investigate the same, with the permission to open it should it prove to be of interest—as was kindly granted in the case of the discovery of Queen Hatshepsut in 1916?

Believe me,
Dear Sir,
Yours faithfully,
Signed: HOWARD CARTER.

No. 33 F. Service des Antiquités, Direction Générale,
Pièces jointes 3 Le Caire, le 8 Décembre, 1918

MONSIEUR

J'ai l'honneur de vous envoyer ci-joint, en double exemplaire, l'autorisation acccordée à Lord Carnarvon pour ouvrir, fouiller et publier le tombeau dont vous avez découvert l'entrée dans la grande vallée au nord de la Vallée des Rois.

Je vous serai obligé de vouloir bien me retourner un exemplaire dûment signé.

Je vous envoie, également pour signature et retour, le double de l'autorisation de la Vallée des Rois.

Veuillez agréer, Monsieur, l'assurance de ma considération distinguée.

Le Directeur Général.
Signé: P. LACAU.

Monsieur Howard Carter, Meir

[No. 33 F. General Direction, Antiquities Service
3 enclosures Cairo, 8th December, 1918.

SIR,

I have the honour to send you a duplicate of the authorization granted to Lord Carnarvon to open, clear and publish the tomb of which you have discovered the entrance in the great valley to the north of the Valley of the Kings.

I would be obliged if you would return to me the original duly signed.

I am also enclosing, for signature and return, the duplicate of the authorization relating to the Valley of the Kings.

Please be assured, Sir, of my distinguished consideration.

The Director General.
Signed: P. LACAU

Mr Howard Carter, Meir]

MINISTÈRE DES TRAVAUX PUBLICS 65
SERVICE DES ANTIQUITÉS

Le Comte de Carnarvon est autorisé à ouvrir, fouiller et publier un tombeau dont l'entrée a été découverte par Mr. Carter dans la grande vallée au nord de la Vallée des Rois.

Les conditions de cette autorisation sont les mêmes que celles qui ont été fixées pour sa concession voisine de la Vallée des Rois, sauf la modification suivante portant sur l'Article 9:

'Art. 9. Les tombes des Rois, Princes, Reines, Grands Prêtres trouvées *intactes* et tous les objets qu'elles renfermeront seront attribués sans aucun partage à notre Musée. Mais s'il s'agit de la tombe *intacte* d'un *particulier,* il est convenu que le Service des Antiquités donnera à Lord Carnarvon un objet important de cette tombe.'

Par les mots 'tombe intacte' employés dans l'autorisation antérieure et ici même, il est bien convenu qu'il ne faut pas entendre une tombe absolument *inviolée*, mais bien une tombe contenant encore son mobilier en bon état et formant un tout, même si les voleurs sont déjà entrés pour prendre les bijoux comme dans la tombe du père et de la mère de la Reine Táia [Tiye].

Les Articles 8 et 10 restent les mêmes.

Le travail sera exécuté par Mr. Carter, qui peut commencer de suite.

Fait en double, au Caire, le 8 Décembre, 1918.

Le Directeur Général du Service des Antiquités,
Signé: P. LACAU.

Vu et accepté la présente autorisation,
LE PERMISSIONNAIRE.
Signed: HOWARD CARTER,
For the Earl of Carnarvon.

[*MINISTRY OF PUBLIC WORKS*
ANTIQUITIES SERVICE

The Earl of Carnarvon is authorized to open, clear and publish the tomb of which the entrance has been discovered by Mr. Carter in the large valley to the north of the Valley of the Kings.

The conditions of this authorization are the same as those which have been agreed upon for the neighbouring concession in the Valley of the Kings, apart from the following modification to Article 9:

'Article 9. Tombs of Kings, Princes, Queens, High Priests found intact *and all the objects which they contain will be allocated to our Museum. But if it relates to an* intact *tomb of a* private person, *it is agreed that the Antiquities Service will give Lord Carnarvon an important object from this tomb.'*

By the words 'intact tomb' used in the previous authorization and also here, it is agreed that it should not mean a tomb absolutely unviolated, *but rather a tomb still containing its furniture in good condition and forming a whole, even if robbers have already entered the tomb to take jewels as in the tomb of the father and mother of Queen Táia [Tiye].*

Articles 8 and 10 remain unchanged.

The work will be carried out by Mr. Carter, who may start immediately.

Made in duplicate, in Cairo, 8th December, 1918.

The Director General of the Antiquities Service,
Signed P. LACAU.

Seen and accepted the present authorization,
THE PERMITTEE.
Signed: HOWARD CARTER,
for the Earl of Carnarvon.]

The disinterring of this document at the present moment is a somewhat disingenuous attempt on the part of the Department to prejudice the terms of Lord Carnarvon's original concession.

In this authorization, which was of a purely temporary nature, and had nothing to do with the Valley of the Kings, a clause is added containing a somewhat fanciful definition of the term 'tombe intacte', and the claim is made that this definition must be held to apply to the Valley Concession also.

It certainly never occurred to Mr. Carter at the time that, by signing this temporary authorization, he could in any way be prejudicing the real Valley Concession; and in any case the Government's contention cannot now hold, the authorization being for one year only, and at the end of that year becoming null and void. No modification or addition was inserted in the Valley Concession, either in the year in which the temporary authorization was issued, or in the subsequent yearly renewals.

APPENDIX II 66

In the light of the full documentary evidence given above, the Government version of the events of the past year is not without interest.

Detailed comment is unnecessary, but it should be noted that the sole cause of the incidents of the first year was Lord Carnarvon's contract with *The Times*, and that the new difficulties at the resumption of the work were raised, not by Mr. Carter, but by the Department itself, as a result, as letters from Departmental officials expressly state (see letters from Mr. Quibell on page 18 and from Mr. Tottenham on page 84), of influence brought to bear on the Government by correspondents hostile to *The Times* contract.

OFFICIAL VERSION OF THE DISPUTE

EXTRACT FROM *THE TIMES*, FEB. 22ND, 1924. (FROM OUR CORRESPONDENT)

The Ministry of Public Works this evening issued the following *communiqué:—*

'Various incidents arose between Mr. Carter and the Antiquities Service last year during the lifetime of the late Lord Carnarvon, but were all smoothed over, thanks to the good sense and courtesy of the regretted late Lord Carnarvon.

'On the death of the latter the Antiquities Service requested the Egyptian Government to authorize Lady Carnarvon to complete the work in the tomb, thus welcoming the widow's very natural desire and assuring the continuity of the scientific research. It was in these conditions and for these reasons that the new authorization in

Lady Carnarvon's name was delivered for the year ending November 1, 1924.

'Simultaneously with the resumption of the work in October of last year new difficulties were raised. Generally the Government's control, even in the mildest form, with the utmost courtesy and within the limits prescribed by the permit, appeared to Mr. Carter to be an annoyance, in which he pretended to find an obstacle to the work.

'It was thus that the right of the publication of the scientific results and the right of ownership of the objects found—defined, as regards the first, by usage, and, as regards the second, by the terms of the permit—were the subject of altogether unforeseen discussions.

'Recently, on the occasion of the opening of the sarcophagus, it appeared necessary to fix the exact programme. Mr. Carter came to discuss it with the Minister of Public Works, and signed an agreement, in which it was
67 stipulated, among other things, that all visits should be
suspended until [a date not specified], and resumed on a date and in an order to be settled later. This agreement was published in a *communiqué* to the Press.'

Flagrantly contravening this agreement, of which every and the slightest detail had been carefully discussed, Mr. Carter expressed the intention of allowing visits to the tomb otherwise than as laid down in the agreement.

The Minister, to his regret, had to hold Mr. Carter to the agreement. Mr. Carter took as an insult this postponement of the visits unforeseen by the programme, and posted in a Luxor hotel a protest couched in inadmissible language, closed the tomb, and declared that the work would not be resumed.

Despite such attitude of Mr. Carter, the Ministry, with the view solely to the interests of science, summoned Mr.

Carter to carry out the programme and resume the work without delay. Mr. Carter's only reply was a demand for apologies and for the cessation of all obstacles and interference, and, before the expiry of the time limit given him, he began legal proceedings against the Government.

On its side the Ministry annulled the permit directly the time limit expired.

The responsibility for the situation thus created rests exclusively on Mr. Carter.

68

APPENDIX III

A new concession has been recently offered to Almina Countess of Carnarvon.

The terms set out below will illustrate the nature of the demands which the Department tried to impose upon Mr. Carter during the past season's work, and are left to speak for themselves. It was, moreover, stipulated by the Government that the four following prerequisite Conditions or Declarations must be signed by Mr. Carter and the other parties concerned as plaintiffs in the legal action against the Egyptian Government in the Tomb matter before the concession would be delivered, viz.:—

1. Renunciation of any right of legal action, claim, or pretension as regards the Tomb of Tut·ankh·amen, or any further right beyond those conveyed by the concession.

2. Desistance from any legal action pending, and an authorization to annul (*rayer*) the pending action.

3. Signing latest (third) formula of apology.

4. Signing by Mr. Carter a declaration to abstain from discourteous language toward the Egyptian Government.

TERMS OF PROPOSED NEW CONCESSION

The General Director of the Department of Antiquities,

Having seen the resolution of the Committee of Egyptology under date of the ....

Considering that difficulties have arisen between the Egyptian Government and Howard Carter, the representative of Lady Carnarvon, in connexion with the excavations carried out in the tomb of Tout·Ankh·Amon in the Valley of the Kings at Luxor, by virtue of the authorizations of 1915 and 1918, granted to Lord Carnarvon, and that of 1923 to Lady Carnarvon;

Seeing that the Government in pursuance of Article 13 of the authorization of 1915, cancelled the authorization for excavation granted to Lady Carnarvon and took the necessary steps for safeguarding the antiquities;

That it informed Lady Carnarvon thereof, declaring to her at the same time that it was willing to grant her a new authorization safeguarding the authority and the rights of the State as well as the scientific interest of the investigations;

That Mr. Carter, on the other hand, sued the Egyptian 69
Government in his name, in the name of the estate of Lord Carnarvon, and in the name of Lady Carnarvon, both in Chambers, in order to secure order appointing him custodian of the Tomb, and before the Judge on the main issue in order to obtain authority to continue the examination and scientific records which he might think necessary of the contents of the Tomb, and to cause to be allotted to the estate of the late Lord Carnarvon one-half of the objects found in the Tomb;

Seeing that all the plaintiff parties in the aforesaid action have since acknowledged that they have no claim to make in connexion with the measures taken by the Government;

That Lady Carnarvon has asked for the issue of a new authorization with a view to continuing the work interrupted in the Tomb of Tout·Ankh·Amon;

That the Egyptian Government, imbued with the desire to ensure the continuation of the scientific work, has no objection to granting this authorization for the next season;

Issues to Lady Carnarvon, on the clauses and conditions hereinbelow set out, the present authorization.

CLAUSE 1

Lady Carnarvon, hereinafter called the beneficiary, is authorized to continue the clearance of the Tomb of Tout·Ankh·Amon situate in the Valley of Kings at Luxor and indicated in the plan hereto annexed;

The authorization is personal. It cannot in any case and in any form be transferred, in whole or in part, to anyone.

It is furthermore issued at the exclusive risk and peril of the beneficiary, without any responsibility on the part of the Egyptian Government.

CLAUSE 2

The present authorisation is given for a period of one year, beginning from 1st November, 1924, and reaching its expiry on 31st October, 1925.

CLAUSE 3

Mr. Carter is appointed by the beneficiary for the direction of the works.

He shall represent the beneficiary on the spot for the purpose of observance of the clauses of the present authorization.

Any change in the person entrusted with the direction of the works shall only be effective if it is accepted in writing by the General Director of the Department of Antiquities.

The beneficiary undertakes not to engage or retain on the staff of the works any person who is not approved by the Minister of Public Works, or whom the latter might subsequently require to be excluded.

70 The Department of Antiquities may nominate one or several persons, to the number of five at most, to carry out their scientific apprenticeship in the said work.

CLAUSE 4

Access to the area of the works is reserved to the staff of the beneficiary, to the officers of the Department of Antiquities, and to the persons referred to in the last paragraph of the preceding article. The Ministry of Public Works reserves to itself the exclusive right of issuing permits to any other person for collective or individual visits.

A number of permits not exceeding ...... per month shall be placed at the disposal of the beneficiary to admit Egyptologists visiting Luxor to the excavation area in case of urgency. The list of these visitors will be communicated monthly to the Department of Antiquities.

CLAUSE 5

The Department of Antiquities shall exercise over the excavation area, through the medium of its officers, its right of supervision and checking both from the point of view of the safety and conservation of the places and the objects found, and from the point of view of the scientific conduct of the works. The beneficiary shall execute the instructions which she shall receive in that connexion from the Department of Antiquities, and shall, on the other hand, not oppose any obstacle to the execution of the measures which this Department might think it necessary to take direct.

It is now straightway prohibited for the beneficiary to take wet paper dabbings from the coloured manuscripts.

CLAUSE 6

The beneficiary, after having examined the objects found, and taken such notes as she may think necessary, shall deliver over the said objects as soon as demand to that effect shall be made to her by the Department of

Antiquities, to the Inspector of that Department or to any other officer appointed for that purpose.

In any case, all objects must be handed over on the expiry of the present authorization.

CLAUSE 7

The beneficiary is bound to draw up a report indicating the features (particulars) observed at the time of opening of any part of the tomb, sarcophagus, coffer, etc., and the place occupied by each object, appending thereto photographs and drawings. These reports shall be communicated to the Department of Antiquities within a reasonable time.

CLAUSE 8

No construction may be put up on the land, the use of which is granted under the present authorization, without a special permission in writing of the General Director of the Department of Antiquities and on the conditions which shall be stipulated therein.

71 Any structure erected in contravention of the present provision shall be immediately demolished by the beneficiary, failing which it will be demolished by the Department at the expense, risk, and peril of the beneficiary, the whole without prejudice to any other penalty.

CLAUSE 9

In the course of the works, the beneficiary is bound to hand to the Department of Antiquities, every week at least (or at shorter intervals to be fixed by that Department), a bulletin setting forth the state of the work.

The beneficiary shall have no exclusive right of publication in the Press of news relating to the works, and the government may at any time publish communiqués or information on this subject in the Press or otherwise.

The beneficiary undertakes not to give any information to the Press before having handed over the bulletin provided in the last preceding paragraph, and not to grant any monopoly for the publication of the above news.

CLAUSE 10

The beneficiary of the authorization undertakes to publish the scientific results of the works within the term of five (?) years from expiry of the present authorization. On the expiry of this term the Ministry of Public Works shall be at liberty to take steps for the said publication.

It is understood that this reservation of scientific publication entails no limitation of the right of the Department of Antiquities to affix on the objects exhibited in the Museum, and to publish in the guides or official bulletins at any time, brief historical or descriptive notices dealing with the objects in question.

The beneficiary further undertakes to deliver free of charge and without expense to the Egyptian Government two copies of the drawings, papers, separate impressions or collections of engravings which might be published by her or her agents on the Tomb of Tout·Ankh·Amon and its contents.

CLAUSE 11

The right of commercial reproduction of the objects found in the course of the works is reserved to the Egyptian Government.

CLAUSE 12

The Tomb of Tout·Ankh·Amon and all the antique

objects coming therefrom shall be reserved in their entirety to the Public Domain of the State. The beneficiary cannot claim any division or allotment of objects on any ground and to any extent whatsoever.

CLAUSE 13

The beneficiary, when the work is terminated, is bound to restore to a satisfactory condition the places and spots occupied by her by virtue of the present authorization.

72 CLAUSE 14

In case of any breach by the beneficiary or her agents of the conditions above set forth, or the orders and instructions given in pursuance of the said conditions, the Minister of Public Works may by simple order, and without any previous notice or formality, pronounce the cancellation of the present authorization.

In that case the Department of Antiquities shall by administrative procedure immediately have all work discontinued, and take all such measures as it may consider necessary, both in the interests of the State and for safeguarding the monuments or objects found, without the beneficiary or any of her agents being entitled to any indemnity or compensation whatsoever of any kind.

APPENDIX IV 73

Since Mr. Carter's return to England, an incident reflecting on his integrity has occurred, which throws some further light on the Egyptian Government's attitude towards him.

London, April 7th, 1924.

TOMB OF TUT·ANKH·AMEN

PAINTED WOODEN HEAD

MY DEAR WINLOCK,

The following copies are in confirmation of the two cables, April 2nd and 3rd, received, and my cabled reply, April 3rd:—

Luxor, April 2, 1924.

Transmit Carter. To be kept confidential.

Egyptian Government Committee have found behind No. 4 (Store Room) in case Fortnum Mason statue head-piece capital unlabelled. Send all the information you can relating to origin. Advise us by letter if any inquiry is made. We shall be prepared. Made a bad impression on Egyptian members. It was announced by telegram to Zaghlool immediately and sent by express Cairo. Lacau and Engelbach have suggested to them you have bought [it] for account of Earl last year from Amarna. Do not know whether they believe that actually.

WINLOCK.

Luxor, April 3, 1924.

Apparently at the request of Lacau, Edgar [and] Engelbach called to-day and have suggested Carter confirm the purchase of head. Thus can give great assistance to Lacau, who has great confidence in him and desires, if possible, to prevent an attempt made by Press to misrepresent Carter. They suggest Quibell should be informed by me. Have been informed by servant voluntarily he made a mistake in storing empties. Code very difficult.

WINLOCK.

(To Winlock.) London, April 3, 1924.

Your cables, second [and] third April, regarding objects of tomb in No. 4, received. The piece mentioned belongs, like all other pieces belonging tomb in No. 4 (Store Room), to material found in filling of passage. They are noted in plan in group numbers, but not yet fully registered in index. Do you wish further details by letter?

HOWARD.

74 As you will have learnt by my cable, the object in question—a painted wooden portrait head of Tut·ankh·amen—belongs to the material discovered in the rubbish filling the passage of the tomb of Tut·ankh·amen.

When I first discovered the tomb and cleared the passage, which was completely filled with rubbish from floor to ceiling between the first and second sealed doorways, I found in that filling a number of objects, whole and broken, which threw light on the history of the tomb after the burial of the King.

These objects were collected under sequence-group numbers, and were stored for eventual study, recording and treatment in Tomb No. 4. Tomb No. 4 was the only magazine for the safe keeping of antiquities I had up to that stage of our work in the Valley, and I should note that it was not until the opening of the Antechamber of the tomb of Tut·ankh·amen that the magnitude of our discovery was realized, and to cope with it I applied for, and

Two large fragments from the stamped blocking of the tomb's outer doorway, probably photographed in the entrance to the tomb of Ramesses XI (KV4) which Carter employed as a storeroom during the early stages of the clearance. Pierre Lacau's discovery in this storeroom of a unique wooden head of Tutankhamun (page 148 and front cover), hidden in a Fortnum and Mason's crate similar to that in the photograph, was a great blow to Carter's credibility. [Griffith Institute, Oxford]

received from the Antiquities Department, permission to use Tomb No. 15 as a storeroom and laboratory. Consequently all objects pertaining to the excavation up to the date of the opening of the Antechamber were stored in Tomb No. 4.

PAINTED AND GESSOED WOODEN HEAD OF TUTANKHAMUN RISING FROM A LOTUS, IN A METAPHOR OF REBIRTH. [GRIFFITH INSTITUTE, OXFORD.]

The disposition of these objects was recorded under sequence-group numbers on the plan made by Messrs. Hall and Hauser, season 1922-23, but many of them await their final recording, photographing and treatment.

This actual piece in question, the most important object found at that stage of the work, was discovered in a very perishable condition, and it took Mr. Callender and myself some little time to salvage it, as well as fallen fragments of its painted decoration, from the rubble and dust. It was carefully packed and immediately stored in Tomb No. 4, with the fragments belonging to it in a separate parcel, and left there till the opportunity came for its correct handling.

I am at a loss to understand such a procedure on the part of the Department as sending it 'by express Cairo', before it had received the proper treatment for transport, and I most sincerely trust that the fragments salvaged by us have received proper care. It would be deplorable if this wonderful and unique portrait-head of the young King has suffered damage through such extraordinary action.

Yours ever,

Signed: HOWARD CARTER.